OUR STORY

BRUCE FOXTON & RICK BUCKLER

Published by:
Castle Communications Plc
Book Division
A29 Barwell Business Park
Leatherhead Road
Chessington
Surrey KT9 2NY

Copyright © 1993 Castle Communications Plc

Bruce & Rick are represented by
The Engine Room, 116 Cleveland Street, London W1P 5ND

Printed in England by J.H. Haynes & Co

ISBN. 1 898141 10 X

THE JAM

Most R&R Maximum R&B

Appearing at

THE GREYHOUND

FULHAM PALACE ROAD

20th MARCH 1976

BE THERE!

UNWIN BROTHERS LIMITED, THE GRESHAM PRESS, OLD WOKING, SURREY

OUR STORY

WRITTEN BY
BRUCE FOXTON
& RICK BUCKLER
WITH ALEX OGG

CONTENTS

FORWARD

The Jam were the quintessential English band. Emerging from the punk explosion of the 1970's, they were a three piece of almost indescribable power and aggression. But while their contemporaries fell by the wayside, they grew into the most successful British band of the time. The reason for this is simple, they had songs. Three minute masterpieces that succinctly mirrored the age. These were not songs 'full of sound and fury, signifying nothing', these were classic anthems that captured the emotion. And seventeen consecutive British hit singles was the result.

Bruce and Rick now, in conjunction with Alex Ogg, for the first time, recount the rise and fall of The Jam.

This is their story.

PHOTO CREDITS

Back Cover..........Paul Canty, Courtesy of London Features Int.
Page 3..Courtesy of Bruce & Rick
Page 13..............Elaine Bryant, Courtesy of London Features Int.
Page 49..Courtesy of Bruce & Rick
Page 50..Courtesy of Bruce & Rick
Page 51..Courtesy of Bruce & Rick
Page 52..Courtesy of Bruce & Rick
Page 53
Top..Courtesy of Barry Plummer
Bottom......................................Courtesy of London Features Int.
Page 54..Courtesy of Bruce & Rick
Page 55
Top..................................Courtesy of London Features Int.
Bottom..Courtesy of Barry Plummer
Page 56..Courtesy of Bruce & Rick
Page 57..Courtesy of Bruce & Rick
Page 58..Courtesy of Mark Paytress
Page 59..Courtesy of Bruce & Rick
Page 60..Courtesy of Bruce & Rick
Page 61
Top..Courtesy of Bruce & Rick
Bottom......................................Courtesy of London Features Int.
Page 62
Top..Courtesy of London Features Int.
Bottom..........Janet Macoska - Courtesy of London Features Int.
Page 63...........Elaine Bryant - Courtesy of London Features Int.
Page 64......................................Courtesy of London Features Int.
Page 113......................................Courtesy of London Features Int.
Page 114......................................Courtesy of London Features Int.
Page 115......................................Courtesy of London Features Int.
Page 116......................................Courtesy of London Features Int.
Page 117......................................Courtesy of London Features Int.

The JAM

The JAM

BRUCE   PAUL   RICK

Introduction

Woking is a grey dormitory town in Surrey, with most its population commuting to London, and a strong divide between middle and working class encampments. Paul Weller was born in the latter on May 25th 1958. He grew up, the son of a featherweight champion boxer and cleaner mother, in a Victorian terrace in Stanley Road. His father, John, was featured on the title sequence to 'Grandstand' at one point, but spent much of his working life on a building site or driving taxis.

Early musical enlightenment arrived for Paul when his mother took him to see an Elvis Presley film. So overwhelmed was he by the King that he took to dancing in the aisles. His Beatles fixation would come slightly later, shortly after he was presented with a guitar from his father one Christmas. John Weller soon noticed his devotion to the instrument.

School was to prove a crushing blow for Paul, who instinctively rejected its convention and austerity. His one solace was a friend called Steve Brookes, who shared Weller's interest in 60s bands like the Kinks and Beatles, and his disinterest in all matters academic. Another reference point was his tentative ambition to play the guitar. Steve was born one day later than Paul, and had a nomadic and unsettled childhood. He arrived at Sheerwater School in Christmas 1971, and was introduced to Paul by mutual

The JAM

friend Roger Pilling.

Paul's father was immediately supportive of the fledgling duo. As soon as he cottoned on to what was happening he booked them into a gig at Woking's Working Men's Club. It was November 1972, and they played Simon & Garfunkel style, an acoustic, six song set with some original lyrics from Paul and Steve. There was an early fashion statement too, with orange loon pants and Elvis shirts partially masking the absurdity of the selection of Tom Jones and Donovan covers.

John Weller had pursued one earlier attempt at shaping the fortunes of his son. He had previously organised a soccer team with the express intention of finding a place for Paul to play in it. However, Paul's footballing abilities were somewhat inferior to those of his team-mates, who were otherwise quite successful. Both father and son decided to plough a different furrow.

With music, Paul had discovered his muse. He and Steve became practically inseparable, practising relentlessly in Paul's bedroom, or walking the streets at five in the morning to get inspiration for a new song. Brookes even shared the Weller's house for a while when he had personal difficulties at home. Paul's parents were nothing if not accommodating. However, there were occasions when John's commitment to his son and friends operated at the expense of his personal life. Later, members of the band clearly remember his wife, Ann, shouting from the door: "You go out with those guys again tonight, don't bother coming back". Clearly he was finding it difficult to compress building, taxi driving, his son's band and his personal life in to twenty four hours. Alas for Ann, it wasn't about to get any easier.

Throughout these early days in the Sheerwater classroom,

The JAM

music teacher John Avory's role was pivotal. Seeking to encourage rather than constrain his pupils' nascent talents, it was down to him that many of the young musicians had access to rehearsal space and instruments. In particular, his liberal tolerance of Paul's views and attitudes would have a lasting effect on the young songwriter.

Looking to expand, the duo of Paul and Steve recruited a fellow outcast at Sheerwater Secondary Modern in the shape of Dave Waller. A dedicated 'beatnik', he was encouraged to divert funds from the acquisition of Blues records and cannabis long enough to invest in a guitar. Weller switched to bass, leaving only the drum stool vacant.

Neil 'Bomber' Harris promptly became the untitled band's first drummer during 1972. Originally from the Maybury Estate, he was six years old when his parents bought him his first drum kit for Christmas. Watching Tamla Motown acts on television, he loved to follow the rhythms which propelled those songs. His devotion to his new instrument was obvious, and his parents invested further with drum lessons.

By the age of fourteen Neil no longer needed them. Music teacher John Avory spotted him and immediately enrolled him in his new school band. At the same time, Neil had started to mess about with a couple of friends, Bruce Foxton and Chris Giles. Together they did a couple of small scale performances playing covers of the Shadows and the like. However, when Bruce got his apprenticeship the band dissolved.

Neil was subsequently introduced to the rest of the boys. Together with Paul Weller, Steve Brookes and Dave Waller, they practised in Paul's bedroom. It proved enjoyable, despite the fact that Neil's musicianship was some several notches higher than that of his compatriots. It was obvious too that, in the long term, Neil's proficiency and different musical tastes would lead him elsewhere.

Before the band reached that juncture, Neil would take part in one of the group's major early triumphs. With a cymbal borrowed from Status Quo, Neil and the band were up against the might of local act, Rock Island Line, who had appeared in the David Essex film 'That'll Be The Day'. Having progressed through a qualifying heat in Sheerwater, Paul, Steve and Dave faced Neil on the Woking Community Centre stage. As soon as the song started, all three jumped round to face the audience. It was a visual tour de force, cocksure with youth and untroubled by the ridiculous theatricality of the situation. And the day was theirs, much to the chagrin of Rock Island Line.

Neil would subsequently work once more with Foxton prior to Bruce joining the band. In actual fact, it was he that recommended Bruce when The Jam advertised for a second guitarist. However, it was not only musical differences that dragged Neil away. The actual turning point came when he had to go on holiday while a prestigious youth club gig beckoned. He returned to find himself out of a job. In stepped Rick Buckler.

Neil has remained active in music on a part-time basis. After his spell with what were the foundations of The Jam, he joined a band working night clubs. He was, in fact, approached again by John Weller to replace Rick for a gig at Michael's that his successor could not attend. Already committed to another engagement, Neil did not complete the circle. After a five year fabrication engineering course, he left college to work for his father, later joining a promi-nent dance band. He remains to this day with the same outfit, supporting Cliff Richard and Kenny Ball amongst others. The band work most weekends while Neil, married

The Jam

with two children, is employed in the daylight hours at a school near his home in Byfleet, Surrey.

Rick Buckler was already an accomplished drummer when he was welcomed into the bosom of The Jam. Paul lent him a set of Chuck Berry records to learn, and that served as his rite of passage. As these all followed essentially the same drum patterns, this did not prove too challenging.

Two years the senior of Brookes and Weller, Rick's twin brother Pete was already active in a garage band. The youngest of a family of all-male offspring, Rick was born Paul Richard Buckler on December 6th, 1955, switching to this second name in his teens. His father worked for the post office, before eventually moving on to the telephones, and Rick has two elder brothers; Andrew and John. Rick had previous 'experience' with Impulse, and possesses the most impressive list of part-time occupations before The Jam's breakthrough. He had served time in a fish shop, motor bike warehouse, drawing office, and passed himself off as an electrical inspector.

He gave up his last job when The Jam were offered a three date tour of US air force bases in Germany - which promptly fell through. Later, he quite clearly remembers John Weller telephoning to inform him that the deal had gone through with Polydor. Something of a relief, as from then on 'I needn't worry about a career I hadn't got'.

Of all The Jam's personnel, Rick was in the process of pursuing the most secure academic career, at least until the lure of music dragged him away from his schoolbooks. He even enjoyed the onerous distinction of a Prefect badge. However, after catching Paul and his friend Roger Pilling having a crafty smoke in the toilets, his inclination was to join rather than admonish them. The sense of responsibility Rick would take in to the workplace was already obvious in his youth.

The music room at Sheerwater school had become a meeting point for anyone and everyone who played an instrument. John Avory was happy to leave the students to their dinner-time jams, not interfering as long as the sessions did not become too boisterous. After all, it also kept the participants out of trouble.

Jamming together Weller, Waller, Brookes and Buckler became, naturally enough, The Jam. It was not the first time the name had been coined, but by now the band were beginning to accept it as their destiny. Alternative theories linking the origin of the name to observations over breakfast or the inspiration of outsiders are spurious, as Rick recalls: 'I think it was just because we were jamming at Sheerwater School. I don't think anyone turned around and said, we're The Jam. The only argument we had was because we couldn't think of a name. There were lots of suggestions, but they were all terrible. Even in the early days we thought, what a horrible name, but because we'd been using it, and couldn't think of anything better, it just stuck'.

Rick remembers the school 'drum kit' to be somewhat rudimentary; one snare and a floor tom. But by the time he left Sheerwater Secondary Modern in 1974, John Avory had conjured a brass band out of his pupils. Which caused considerable embarrassment when Rick was volunteered by a friend to replace the troupe's absent regular drummer, Nigel Constable, at a school assembly. Completely unfamiliar with the style of music, Rick found himself struggling manfully to match the tempo changes observed by his colleagues. 'I didn't have a clue what I was meant to be playing. It wasn't very much like Chuck Berry anyway'. It did little to reinforce his 'street cred' either.

The Jam

Rick's own drum kit was 'borrowed' from the Guildford YMCA. Consisting of one cymbal, a snare and bass drum, its purchase was never secured officially, because its owner never bothered to chase him up for payment. Hardly comparable to the way Steve Jones illicitly acquired the Sex Pistols' equipment, perhaps, but a flash of opportunism all the same.

The Jam's first oxygen of exposure with the new line-up misfired in the time honoured tradition of such things. The consumption of large quantities of alcohol to quell pre-gig nerves provided an inauspicious start in front of 40 assembled schoolmates at Sheerwater Youth Club. It was the summer of 1973, and John Weller, now moving into the role of manager, was reportedly none too pleased. An incident logged in various Jam archives, but one in which Rick can only remember 'something about drinking'.

Having set up their instruments, the band had charged into a perfunctory sound check. Unfortunately, the equipment didn't share their enthusiasm. Convinced that it wasn't going to work, the band wandered off to the pub to get steamed in consolation. Only when they returned did they discover that John had found someone to rectify the problems. Which was a bit late, as they were now completely incapable of standing up straight, never mind playing in time.

Typically, The Jam would remember their origins by playing a benefit gig for Sheerwater Youth Club, in Guildford, on April 18 1980. After all, they had borrowed the Youth club van often enough. Paul's gratitude extended as far as gracing the event stoked on sulphates, just to set a good example.

Repaying another instalment on John Weller's investment of time and energy, the band won a second talent contest at the local Kingsfield Social Club. John's policy might have been derived from his old trade analogy of building firm foundations. The idea was that if John could go round showing photographs of nice lads with trousers and matching shirts and ties, they would be perceived as a 'respectable' band. Publicans could book them safe in the knowledge that they could play, unobtrusively, between bingo sessions. Their white bomber jackets, pink shirts and white kipper ties hardly screamed rebellion at prospective booking secretaries.

However, Dave Waller had already had enough, electing instead to move on to a hit or miss career as a poet. 'When it came down to it', recalls Rick, 'he really wasn't that great a guitarist, and he was sort of pushed out when it became obvious he wasn't going to get any better'. Taking the Beatnik lifestyle through to its natural conclusion, he died of a heroin overdose in 1982. Weller had published the first of his books, 'Notes From Hostile Street', on the Riot Stories label in 1979.

Ironically Waller was found dead in a room above the Wheatsheaf Hotel, The Jam's former drinking haunt. The band had known of his descent in to the netherworld of hard drugs, but had been unable to do anything to dissuade him.

Waller is remembered with affection for being the 'goat who got kicked' in the band's early stages. With The Jam for most of their youth club gigs, the prospect of playing working men's clubs was too much for such a staunch idealist. Capable of talking long in to the night, and with overbearing intensity, about Marxism and political theory, his views had a significant influence on Weller's song writing. However, this did not stop Paul from playing mean tricks on him. These included stripping his guitar neck of all its varnish so that it was practically impossible to play. Poor

Dave probably thought the neck was meant to feel like that. His instrumental skills, not surprisingly, are not remembered as being of great import.

By this time, John Weller had managed to coax his son in to an exploratory poke at the building industry. It was a purely temporary aberration. Together with Steve Brookes, John instructed the pair on the traditional method of throwing bricks up, three at a time, to a colleague standing at the top of the scaffolding. Their technique was lamentable; each time having to run for cover as the mis-timed projectiles fell back to the ground. Instead the pair sat around on piles of sand getting a sun tan and smoking.

Steve remembers one occasion when he was stood next to John Weller watching Paul trying to pack some bricks together. It was a pathetic sight. 'Look at that wanker. If he couldn't play the guitar what hope would there be for him' was his father's summary. The two lads were so completely useless, in short, that John Weller quickly put behind him any ideas he may have had about a family business. Not in the building trade at least.

Paul and Steve also tried their hand as window cleaners. They prepared by purchasing the requisite buckets and ladders, and were full of bravado about how they would spend the fortune this would bring them. But this occupation too proved a little arduous. On a summer's day sitting down in the shade and discussing girls and music seemed a far more attractive pursuit than actually working.

It was May 1974 when printer's apprentice Bruce Foxton was drafted in to replace Waller. Formerly of progressive garage band Rita, who had managed two live outings, Bruce was tired of their inability to get out of the scout hall. 'I preferred Rita's style to that of The Jam, which seemed to be loads of dodgy cover versions.' He was asked twice to join, finally relenting because of the prospect of actually doing some live work. Though the gigs they did at that time are remembered as quite 'sickly', covers of 'Blue Moon' notwithstanding, The Jam remained the one local band seen to be moving on.

Bruce Foxton's parents were Londoners, though they had moved out of the capital before his birth, becoming part of the London overspill. His family lived at 126 Albert Drive, Sheerwater, where he was born on the 1st of September 1955. His father worked as a painter and decorator, often for the council, although he would take work 'where he could find it', including the collection of football pools money. His mother was primarily a housewife, though she did work part-time at bakeries and the like. Bruce has two elder brothers; the eldest Ray, a bus driver, and Derek, who is still involved in the print business.

Bruce was originally a rhythm guitarist, but on Paul's invitation, was encouraged to switch to bass. Steve Brookes recalls that he 'got the hump' about making the switch, though Bruce remembers quite happily giving it a try. It was a logical development; Paul was experiencing difficulty in combining both bass and vocal duties, and Bruce was lucky enough to inherit his venerated Hoffman Violin Bass, purchased by Paul in deference to his hero Paul McCartney. Up until this point, the three-piece had seen Steve Brookes handling lead vocals and guitar. Bruce received instruction in some rudimentary bass lines and the change soon became a permanent one. Eventually, it would allow Paul to pick up the mantle of lead singer when Brookes moved on.

Shortly after Bruce and Paul had swapped instruments, the band came into contact with the record industry proper for the first time. John Weller had been posting demo tapes to every known address in the music industry. Terry Slater, an A&R man at EMI, got them in for an audition. However, their youth and lack of strong original material lay behind his decision to 'let them down gently'.

Bruce received a good deal of flak from his parents as his involvement in the band grew. Following his middle brother's lead, he had joined the printing trade which offered comparatively good prospects. By the tail end of his apprenticeship his employer's patience was wearing thin at his flimsy excuses for late arrivals and absences, but he characteristically saw it through the full five years before making the switch to The Jam.

Despite joining what in essence was a 'covers band', there was at least one further attraction to The Jam. As had become traditional in the working men's club scene, the band were always able to keep the last part of their set to themselves. It was then possible to play the faster and more outrageous material because everybody was too drunk to notice.

The songs written by Weller and Brookes at this stage were weak and embryonic, following a close harmony style which owed far too great a debt to the Beatles. Titles such as 'Forever And Always', one of their first original compositions, have been lost to this period. However, given any opportunity to jump about a bit and show off, both Paul and Steve were up for it. Steve had even managed to learn how to play his guitar behind his back, Hendrix style, to the faster Chuck Berry R&B covers.

Later they would continue to compose original material like 'Lovin' By Letters' and 'More And More'. Steve remembers Paul as being somewhat ahead of him in the songwriting stakes, but both were quick to recognise their own limitations. Whenever they were struck for a decent or interesting chord progression, 'The Complete Beatles

Songbook' was always there for inspiration. Some years later, hearing The Jam go to number one with the explicitly derivative 'Start', Steve was reminded of this technique. Like many fans of the Fab Four, he still maintains that Paul had a bit of a cheek pulling that off.

The atmosphere between the four band members was never easy. With Paul and Steve representing a private clique, and everyone's hormones and egos inflamed by their adolescence, flashpoints were never far from the surface. 'And somehow within the band, we just knew that something wasn't quite right'.

Tapes still exist of some of the early material committed to demos. The working men's clubs dates were used to finance trips to Bob Potter's (the owner of the Lakeside complex) studio. Tapes were mailed off in the hope that London labels might pick up on their burgeoning talents. Terry Slater and EMI aside, it was a vain effort. Although many local bands turned their noses up at the sort of venues The Jam were playing, the constant rehearsing and performance allowed them to make considered progress. The fact that The Jam were not only getting work, but channelling any profits in to recording sessions, had also helped entice Bruce in to the fold.

Still a four piece, the essential ingredients of the band were now in place. They began to advertise themselves under the heading: "The Jam: Maximum R&B".

<u>Prologue</u>

Four Number One singles, over five million world-wide sales, and a fan base as fervent as any the last twenty years have seen. The Jam were the biggest, most important and most credible pop band since the Beatles. But it nearly never happened.

The band had been trawling through the streets of the capital, fly-posting their hand-made leaflets, designed and produced on the sly at the printers where Bruce Foxton was employed. He and Paul Weller had been working together in their pre-appointed areas, while Rick Buckler and John Weller, Paul's father and band manager, took another route. Paul, nominally on look-out duty, failed to intercept the policeman who tapped Bruce on the shoulder. 'Just taking them down, officer', he offered unconvincingly.

Just about satisfied with their day's work, and the fact that Bruce hadn't been arrested, the two pairs assembled back at their cars for the journey home to Woking. The convoy set off down the A3, led by Bruce's Cortina Mark II, Rick and John bringing up the rear in the drummer's battered Mini.

Some way into their journey, Bruce noticed the road narrowing from three lanes to one, cordoned off by huge railway sleepers. Visibility was poor, and the quartet were tired from their days exertions. 'I glanced in my rear mirror, and realised, with mounting horror, that Rick

27

hadn't followed me into the correct channel. It was one of those awful moments where you know something terrible is going to happen but you can't do bugger all to stop it'.

Panic ensued in the following vehicle. John realised the danger a split second before Rick, and made a vain attempt to snatch the wheel to avert collision. His efforts were in vain. The car hit the sleeper, somersaulted over the barrier, and landed back on its wheels opposite a fish and chip shop. A few seconds later the car's occupants came round.

The Recaro seats had held their passengers safely, but the Polyseal they had been using to stick the posters up flew everywhere. John Weller regained consciousness, seriously worried about which part of his body was leaking this foul fluid. Rick was only slightly more lucid, but remembers that 'it took a great deal of effort to convince him that his brains were not coming out'.

The real casualty was Rick himself. 'I'd broken my foot, and I had to be physically carried on for the gig at the Fulham Greyhound, the one which we'd been doing the fly posting for'. There were many in the audience who thought it was a gimmick. It was, however, just another example of the band's total dedication. 'And it bloody well hurt too much to be a gimmick'.

CHAPTER ONE

Any Guitar And Any Bass Drum

The band's early days were characterised by shows at any venue that would book them. One of their more regular local haunts was Michael's in Woking. The proprietor, Hermes, took The Jam on as his resident house band after they passed an audition on the 22nd of January 1974. Of course, Michael's wasn't much to look at, even from the inside. Little more than a tatty late night drinking hole, its other 'turn' was a regular strippers' spot.

The management made the mistake of letting their resident house band record there one evening. When they returned they found the boys had drunk the bar dry. 'Well,' remembers Rick, 'we were originally just going to have a little sip out of each bottle, but you can imagine how that turned out. We weren't very restrained in those days'.

Although they were allowed to continue to rehearse and play at the venue, Hermes and his assistant Pepe made sure that all the relevant bottles were marked up in future. But it wasn't just alcohol that was keeping the boys' minds off their work. Paul had discovered that if you walked up the fire escape, you could see the strippers' dressing room. Such divine knowledge was imparted to his colleagues, and the message trickled down through their circle of friends. For a couple of weeks Michael's was not only their only regular booking, but also a free peek-show. The night they were discovered the fire escape was all but collapsing under the sheer weight of numbers. 'I suppose we got a little over ambitious' reflects Bruce. 'We should each have taken turns or two at a time, but everyone's hormones got the better of them'.

Michael's was a tough club. One night when the band were playing there a gentleman was denied entry to his favourite premises. He returned a few short minutes later and blew the whole of the front door away with a shotgun. 'It was that kind of clientele'.

Due to licensing laws, the door staff would refuse entry to anyone who was not wearing a tie. In consequence, a huge carrier bag full of old ties was kept next to the door and hired out to casual punters. In tribute, Paul Weller played one set at the joint wearing nothing but a collar, cuffs and tie. As a fashion statement the idea was neat, but somewhat ahead of its time. Or, as Rick succinctly states, 'He looked a bit of a prat really, but at least they looked up from their pints'. Whatever, the boys enjoyed playing there, and it did pay a fiver each and every Saturday.

At the same time as they were playing Michael's the band were booked for a gig at Bunters in Guildford; 'a horrid discotheque style joint'. The Jam had pulled a support slot to Rock Island Line, the relatively popular glam rock act of the parish. They still resented The Jam for having robbed them of the talent contest award a year previously. The band set up their equipment, ran through a cursory sound check, and went home. It was a particularly big night for Bruce, who had not long been a member of the band: 'I had arranged to meet my friends at the nearby Horse & Groom, further up the high street'. However, the calendar date was

The JAM

to become one of the most infamous in the history of Guildford. October 5, 1974 was the night of the IRA bombings.

The Horse & Groom was one of two pubs blown apart. Bruce found the street closed off, and was turned away by the police. 'I was forced to go home with the rest of the band, who were later telephoned and told the gig was off. Which hardly came as a surprise considering the circumstances. But I had my mates to worry about too, and nobody really had a clue what was going on'. Unbeknown to him, his friends had left the scene uninjured after crawling out of a shattered window. By the morning he knew of their safety, leaving the band free to return to Bunters to retrieve their equipment. It is not an incident remembered with any fondness at all either by Bruce or the rest of the band.

They returned the equipment to its usual resting place. During these early days the boys gear was stored in a lock-up garage in Horsell, just outside their local ale house, the Wheatsheaf. 'However', remembers Bruce, 'the site had severe drainage problems. Consequently John Weller had to arrange to borrow wooden pallets to place the instruments on, a few feet above water level'. All in all it made a captivating little display.

Other early gigs included rounds of the cabaret circuit, weddings, and 21st birthday parties. One early coup was a gig at Chelsea Football Club on the 21st of April, 1975, for which the band received the princely sum of £55. Other less likely, and less lucrative venues, included the Hindehead British Legion Club, Sheerwater Fete, HM Prison Coldingly, and even a Police Ball. 'I remember playing down the bill to drag acts, strippers, you name it' recounts Rick, whose diary of the time recalls the accounts for 1974: 88 gigs, earning a total of £1,657.

The JAM

John Weller worked hard on the band's behalf. Whatever was needed to keep the band gigging would be provided by him. This resulted in a bewildering array of transport solutions. Comfortably the most bizarre of these was a big Luton transit van they had to share with the owner's pet.

'We were a bit unprepared for this', is Bruce's choice understatement. 'John Weller had been smirking a bit, and so had the driver. We thought we'd open up the back and there would be a hole in the floor or something. After all, that sort of thing wasn't unusual. So anyway, we pulled open the doors, and there, sat in the corner, peering back, is this bloody huge lion. I think it must have thought it was feeding time'.

One of John's friends from the building trade had owned the animal, actually a lioness, since it was a cub. But it was now too large to keep in the house because it kept eating the furniture. So it lived inside his Luton van, and if you wanted to borrow the vehicle, fine, but the lioness came with it. The vehicle was thus loaded up with guitars and amplifiers by a succession of shaky hands desperately trying not to offend its occupant.

In transit the musical equipment was stored under the lion's watchful gaze. On arrival, band members carefully removed their instruments ('Bloody carefully' nods Rick) and made their way out for a typical club performance. Loading up afterwards, an employee of the club offered the band a hand to lug their gear back to the van. 'Well, we'd had it done to us, so we couldn't really resist it....' The Jam entourage innocently pointed out the white Luton and left him to open up.

The hapless volunteer made his way over, and unlocked the rear doors. He stood there, stock still, for about two seconds, before turning round, dropping the amp he was

The Jam

holding, and bolting off in the opposite direction. It did not occur to him to ask for an explanation. 'We were stood back at the pub, and you could sort of picture an invisible cartoon bubble appearing above the guy's head saying something along the lines of "Fucking hell, there's a lion in the back of this van". Which was exactly the situation we'd been in about an hour earlier'.

So The Jam joined with the animal's owner in the front of the vehicle. While enjoying the trip home, a huge furry paw landed on John Weller's shoulder. 'Of course, we froze again. But the lion's owner simply turned round and smacked it straight on the nose'. Despite being a full grown, king of the jungle, it was actually fairly tame. 'Legend has it', continues Rick, 'that the lioness was eventually retired to a park zoo, after it attempted to sexually assault a young woman wearing a fur coat'.

Luton vans with large carnivores inside were not the only transport problems to be dealt with. Another time they travelled to Folkestone in a Dormobile that was some way short of road-worthy. On a freezing winter night, with holes peppering the bodywork, the band arrived at their destination barely able to feel their limbs. 'It was getting to the point where we'd had enough really', Rick shivers at the thought. 'This was about the same time John Weller was mulling over the possibilities of converting an old ambulance, which might have come in handy at some of those early gigs'. In the meantime, anything with four wheels that could move remained a legitimate target for requisition by John Weller.

One of their final gigs at Sheerwater Community Centre made the band decide that a move into the London circuit was now overdue. They were beginning to create their own sound, and the lack of response was inhibiting. Despite their increasing proficiency, club goers in Woking were never going to be that appreciative of anything beyond a competent rendition of 'Yesterday'. 'We were beginning to get tired of playing original material to an older audience sitting motionless, with fingers planted firmly in their ears'.

They caught a similar reaction at their final booking at Woking Liberal Club, on the 23rd of March 1975. The whole event ended in a physical fight with the venue's committee. Steve Brookes, customarily worse for wear, had decided it would be a good idea to dance on the piano, while continuing to strum along. The committee members were appalled at seeing their keyboard desecrated by the young upstarts, and made their feelings known to him. At first this was merely a request. Steve was having none of it. They then decided to physically remove him. As Rick recalls, the whole event soon descended in to farce: 'Unfortunately for the committee, Steve was having far too much fun to stop. The width of the piano gave him enough room to scuttle to the other side while the committee members ran around. And when they got to the other side of the piano he would run back again. That was the last time we played there. Hardly surprising really'.

Bruce had played his first major gig at the Croydon Greyhound in November 1974, supporting Thin Lizzy. Only knowing approximately four or five of the songs, Bruce hovered in the wings until making his entrance for the second half of the set. John Weller had hassled the venue for the slot through an old boxing contact. The support was a significant boost, even if they did only receive a fiver between them. The headlining band were very encouraging to the youngsters sharing their dressing rooms. Which was considerate in the circumstances, as The Jam looked more like an 'Opportunity Knocks' cabaret act than hard rockers. 'They were pretty friendly, though I'm sure they wondered who the hell had booked us'.

By the time John Weller got them another support at the same venue, this time to Stackridge, on the 6th of July 1975, Steve Brookes was on the verge of departure. Brookes frustration was compounded when he damaged a finger lifting equipment. The fact that Stackridge's fans indulged in mindless turnip throwing throughout the gig (a Dorset gimmick apparently) didn't help. He went off to play solo sets in wine bars, and fulfilled a personal ambition by setting up the Abacorn Music shop in Brookwood. The Jam came down en masse to have a pint with him and wish him good luck.

Weller and Brookes had previously been the most intimate of friends, a close partnership to which the rest of The Jam were not privy. This was particularly true for Bruce. 'I always felt like an outsider, the new kid on the block in the early stages'. The split between Weller and Brookes resembled the break-up of lovers; from being as 'Thick As Thieves', a partnership recalled on the song of the same name, they stopped socialising completely. A parting of the ways which would mirror The Jam's eventual dissolution.

Brookes remembers their differences as being largely musical. Steve wanted to continue with poppy material, while Paul was beginning to inject a harsher, 'mod' edge to his songs. Their relationship became strained partially because Paul was such an 'all or nothing' merchant. Dogmatic and temperamental, the young Weller was a perfectionist and unlikely to surrender artistic control to Steve when their views clashed. Though they were great friends, Paul came from an enormously different background. Whichever way he might have looked at it, unlike Steve, Paul was constantly indulged by his parents. Consequently he was used to getting his own way.

Another factor which may have helped end their creative and social relationship was that fact that Steve had latterly found a steady girlfriend, and secured a job humping furniture for a removal company. Paul simply could not deal with any compromise in commitment to the band. Not unless it was his compromise anyway.

For all the band's later success, Steve would never seriously regret leaving, and assiduously renounces the 'Pete Best Of The Jam' tag. After playing club sets solo until he was twenty, he decided that he was never going to be an adequate career musician. The music shop eventually closed too, due to exchange rates between America and England no longer favouring imports. He moved on to selling cars, his profession to this day.

A couple of auditions were staged for replacements. Bruce remembers that: 'Paul's love of the Beatles led him to believe that a four-piece was the ideal rock 'n' roll platform'. They were committed to doing three shows at Working Men's clubs, and wanted to fill out the line-up in time for these. It was the 9th of July 1975 when the advert appeared, reading, simply; "Jam require lead guitarist". Brian Viner and Pete Jessop replied. The latter actually worked out quite well, and may have been considered as a permanent replacement. However, he never bothered to appear for the scheduled gigs. A note in Bruce's diary recalls the incident: "Well Pete Jessop - cheers mate. We are very annoyed about the whole situation". Although they would later flirt with a keyboard player, from now on they were essentially the trio a nation would come to know as The Jam.

However, unbeknown to either Rick or Bruce, Paul had made a phone call to Steve Brookes to see if he would be interested in rejoining, following some further interest from EMI. Apparently they too had thought the band would only really work as a four-piece.

The
JAM

A final footnote is that one of the songs co-written with Brookes, 'Takin' My Love', would eventually turn up on the b-side to The Jam's debut 'In The City'. Originally a country rock effort, it was subsequently spiced up to new wave tempo. It had been one of two songs recorded, alongside Paul's 'Blueberry Rock', for the band's first demo. Not that Steve ever received any royalties for it.

One month later, on August the 12th, the band were auditioning for a place on television programme 'Opportunity Knocks'. Ann Weller, John's long-suffering wife, had written in advocating the youngster's talents. 'We travelled to a town hall in Surbiton, where we found ourselves surrounded by similar hopefuls. The event was laid out like a fairground, the judges walking around the hall viewing each act. We had our five minutes, before the officials moved on to the neighbouring juggling dog act, or whatever'. The affair is remembered with considerable embarrassment, 'though we were very keen to win it at the time'.

Back at Michael's, the band came their closest to a premature split. Bruce and Rick had enquired about the money they should have received for dates at the venue, while John Weller was explaining what all the expenses were. John took umbrage at what he saw as the suggestion that he was being dishonest. 'He wasn't, of course, its just that things were run on such a tight budget and everybody was struggling to make ends meet'. Paul immediately sided with his father and somehow, over a few coppers, the band had managed to split into two camps.

John Weller immediately recruited older musicians to back Paul on some shows he had lined up. The combination simply did not work. Bruce and Rick discussed the possibility of setting up their own band, 'but we never really got anywhere'. Finally, Rick received a conciliatory phone call from John Weller. 'At that point it just seemed stupid to

The
JAM

lose what was becoming a good thing for all of us'. Within a few days each party had agreed to give it another shot and The Jam were back on track again.

Still on their rounds of working men's clubs, they were introduced to Status Quo's Rick Parfitt one evening. He and 'Pop' Weller frequented the same club, one which Parfitt's father also used. Rick would cherish the mighty wisdom Mr Parfitt shared with him: 'I picked up a useful lesson in the technique of a rock drummer. "When the lead guitar's playing, use the ride cymbal. And when its not, use the high hat". Naturally, I've built my career around that'. Status Quo actually provided more pragmatic help too. Neil Harris had already borrowed a cymbal, and, if The Jam were stuck for an amp or equipment at any stage, John Weller was always able to approach the Parfitts. As Bruce recalls, 'he even attempted to borrow some of Keith Moon's equipment at one point. It was one of the few things he didn't get away with'.

CHAPTER TWO

Boys About Town

Weller had grown up listening to predominantly black music, and throughout gigs at the Fulham Greyhound in 1975, soul cover versions dominated their sets. However, a trip to London in August 1976 would, temporarily, shift his musical perspective. The Sex Pistols played the Lyceum that summer evening, providing Paul Weller with instant enlightenment. Punk was about to take the capital by storm, and with it would come a complete re-assessment of The Jam's musical outlook.

If the Pistols provided the initial spark, it would be the Clash who would politicise The Jam. Strummer said to Weller at the time that everybody should write about things that matter - which is reflected, sometimes quite awkwardly, in many of Paul's early lyrics. Black music and 60s pop would take a back seat for two albums (although early Roxy sets were still filled with revitalised soul numbers like Arthur Conley's 'Sweet Soul Music', Lee Dorsey's 'Ride Your Pony', and Martha and the Vandella's 'Heat Wave') while The Jam channelled their energies in to the aggression of the new wave.

'Our first London dates convinced us that we had to toughen up musically. It was obvious that some of our early attempts at song writing had already become dead-wood. In the working men's clubs you never had to win anyone over; they hadn't come to see the band anyway'. It was a period of transition, and suddenly their audience was placing greater demands on them. The ethos of the growing punk movement also dictated that the cover versions, with one or two notable exceptions, would have to go. Paul was immediately placed under pressure to come up with more of his own, original material.

Hardened against rejection by the club circuit, these early ventures still proved quite intimidating to a young band. The omnipresent John Weller did as much as he could to help whip up support for them. And, if that meant going out into the audience during those early Roxy and Nashville sets and starting the calls for an encore by himself, then so be it.

Despite the furious pace they picked up musically, The Jam's image always reinstated a devotion to the 60s. From the first suits they purchased from Hepworth's in Woking on the 'never never', the visual aspect of The Jam never suggested either punk or new wave. However, they do remember the slightest trace of rebellion in their choices later on. 'In the early 70s we had new suits cut from templates by the tailor. The shop staff could hardly believe it when we told them we only wanted inch wide lapels, and box jackets.'

The man who would become Bruce's best man, Martin Price, witnessed one of the early gigs. 'It was quite funny really. He commented that though the band had potential, they would have to ditch the suits. It was a bit like the guy from Decca turning down the Beatles in retrospect'. Strangely enough, The Jam's eventual producer was actually at those same Beatles sessions. The suits, although they did run against the ethos of the times, certainly helped to

The Jam

differentiate The Jam from a gaggle of lesser bands.

Later in their career, the band discovered a small emporium called Carnaby Cavern, just off Carnaby Street, where they purchased their famous mohair suits. It was several years later before they discovered the shop hid a peephole where a certain member of staff would watch them change. 'That sent a shiver up our spines', winces Bruce.

Allied to their dress sense, one important aspect of the band's sound served a similar purpose: The Jam's faith was fully pledged to the cult of the Rickenbacker (both guitar and bass). Bruce, by nature a guitarist, quite often led the melody lines and picked rather than plucked. This helped to give the band a harder resonance which confirmed their position as part of the new breed, but at the same time the sound of the Rickenbacker tied them to an earlier period.

In October 1976 they took to the streets to play an apparently impromptu gig in Soho market on a Saturday morning. Sponsored by Rock On Records, it was deliberately engineered to give the band maximum exposure. 'The Clash were there to see us, up from their squats for the day', recalls Rick. As was Mark Perry of Sniffin' Glue. It brought them their first, bad review from Caroline Coon in the Melody Maker. The event is remembered with amusement. 'We expected to be moved on by the cops'. However, when said constabulary members merely smiled and tapped their feet at their indulgence, the trio suddenly realised with alarm that they might have to contribute several songs more than they had anticipated, let alone rehearsed. 'We thought we'd at least get dragged away for a night in the cells and some publicity'.

The band also enjoyed a couple of dates at the famous jazz haunt, Ronnie Scott's. At this time the upstairs area was 'a cheesy, low rent drinking hangout', but it still made a nice entry on the band's CV. Having made the progression in to the London circuit, the band were in the process of 'sussing out the most suitable venues for ourselves'.

The Sex Pistols, meanwhile, played a low-profile tour to celebrate signing to EMI. They needed a support band quickly for a date at Queensway Hall, Dunstable, on the 21st of October 1976. John Weller received the phone call and the band were only too pleased to oblige. They very nearly played as a four-piece too. They had already performed once at the 100 Club with a keyboard player Bob Gray. Due to the fact that a huge piano dominated the stage of the venue, this did not prove a problem. However, the logistics of transporting such a huge instrument became untenable, although they had intended to play with their new recruit at the Pistols gig. After a parting of the ways, their would-be accompanist was last spotted when he came backstage after a show in Canada, where he made his home.

In actual fact, Bob Gray's story in almost as interesting as that of The Jam's. Like his former employers, he also appeared in the Guinness Book Of Records. His inclusion is due to his ability to write forwards and backwards with both hands and feet. He can also speak backwards, fluently. Based originally on Sheerwater estate, he was already very keen on conjuring tricks when he met the band. Which, presumably, had something to do with his dexterity on keyboards. When Bruce and Rick went back to his flat in Canada, they learned that he had started out as a magician's apprentice before beginning his own, highly successful, stage show. He took great delight in regaling his former compatriots with his most dazzling spoon bending and card tricks. 'He was very impressive actually.', recalls Bruce, 'he'd obviously made the right career move'.

The band remember the Pistols' performance that October

The Jam

night as a total revolution in their thinking. Aside from Paul, this was their first experience of the group. 'We'd read all these things in the press about them not being able to play a note, that they were just a creation of Malcolm McClaren, and they didn't have any songs. Well they did have some songs, and they were absolutely brilliant'. With only a smattering of an audience, the Pistols' performance was still powerful and fresh. The excitement they generated transmitted naturally to the young pretenders supporting them.

The Jam's impetus was only added to by Caroline Coon's comments in the 'Melody Maker', though the revivalist tag, which she invoked, was hard to shake. The review was cut out on to a piece of cardboard, with the two-fingered retort 'How can I be a fucking revivalist when I'm only 18' scrawled underneath. Paul wore it round his neck on stage, to the bemusement of uninformed audience members. They were equally unafraid of another accusation they faced, that of technical proficiency: Weller went as far as burning a copy of 'Sniffin' Glue' at one gig because it said they spent too long tuning up on stage. 'With those things it was usually Paul who instigated them, but we all went along with them because they were also a great way of getting some publicity. Getting your name in the papers really did help us get gigs too'.

From one-off placements, the band eventually scored their first London residency at the Red Cow, Hammersmith. In the process they pulled their 'own' audience for the first time. But despite punk being in full swing, there were still those who didn't wish to embrace its violent and loud aesthetic. At a typical stint, a curious American wandered in off the street during the sound check. 'He was stood in front of the stage, being really obnoxious. He kept taunting us and shouting that we couldn't play, so we got one of the roadies to pick him up by the scruff of the neck and turf him out. Apparently, when he was outside he kept complaining about the lack of English hospitality'.

Another visitor to the Red Cow, and later gigs at the Marquee, was somewhat more receptive. Chris Parry, A&R man at Polydor, came to see the band for the first time in 1976, on the advice of one Shane McGowan. Then of the Nips, now, sometimes anyway, of the Pogues, he became a massive early fan. His efforts included promoting The Jam through his punk fanzine 'Bondage'. Another early supporter was '48 Thrills' editor Adrian Thrills, who would go on to join the "NME".

Parry saw the raw talent of the band and was quick to predict their potential. He wasn't completely won over, however. For one thing he thought Rick's drumming was too flashy, or flashier than it need be for the songs. His view was that Rick's technique should be more "bossy". 'Which was why, later on, I bought him a T-shirt with "Bossy" written on it'.

Island were interested but dismissed the band as 'not punk enough'. They had also been offered a deal with the independent Chiswick, which amounted to £500 and free use of a PA, but were already thinking of bigger things. The first demo session for Polydor, at Anemone Studios in Brodwick Street, was blown out by an IRA bombing just down the road in Oxford Street. However, after the completion of the session a week later, in February 1977 Polydor eventually coughed up £6000 for their services. They were firmly encouraged by Parry, who was furious that they had let the Clash and Pistols slip through their hands.

The deal was handled by John Weller, though the band simply remember 'Chris Parry waving a lot of contracts in our faces and demanding "Sign this, sign that", but we weren't really about to complain. We were still in our early

20s, or teens in Paul's case, and the Polydor offer amounted to being paid for what we loved doing. The thought of turning it down hardly crossed our minds'. When the news broke, the band received a telegram from Terry Slater at EMI congratulating them. He had obviously seen enough early promise to keep an eye on their progress.

John Weller was clearly out of his depth when it came to handling the record companies. According to Chris Parry, he didn't even want to read the contracts. It was just as well then, that Parry did have the band's interests at heart. The £6,000 figure was as much as he had been able to screw Polydor's MD to. It was still a little embarrassing, however, compared to the figures that were being bandied about among the group's peers.

One final obstacle had to be overcome before The Jam could become Polydor employees. As if to prove just how green they were about the business side of the industry, John Weller had to confess to Parry that they could not cash the cheque. Neither he, Paul, Bruce or Rick had a bank account. The long-suffering Parry had to pay it into his account, and cash the readies for the band.

The contract was merely for one single with an option on an album. But before 'In The City' (among the tracks from the audition demo) was released, Chris Parry walked in to Polydor studios to announce that the label had picked up their option.

'It was just a really exciting time; using decent recording equipment at last being one real novelty'. John Weller immediately went out and spent £1,200 on a completely inappropriate and practically inoperable PA. Paul followed his father's rashness by charging out and buying just about every Rickenbacker guitar he could find. A start had been made on the learning curve.

There was talk from Polydor about getting The Jam aligned to a management company 'proper'. Chris Parry was also interested in continuing his high profile role within the band, but the trio stuck fast behind John Weller. Despite his obvious qualities, a more experienced manager might have held out for a much better deal once his protégés had proven themselves with their first single in the charts. The contract was re-negotiated within 90 days, but it did not drastically improve. At least the royalty rate had changed from the paltry 6% originally offered. If John Weller had a fault as manager, it was simply that he expected everyone around him to act as altruistically as he himself did. The music business did not work like that. The deal from Polydor actually wasn't that good at all, as Rick and Bruce would discover to their cost later in their careers.

The publishing situation offered another considerable drawback for Bruce and Rick. Whereas everything else would be split four ways, the publishing royalties went to the song's author alone. 'On reflection, Rick and myself should have received a percentage of every song. Because even if you're not lyrically contributing, you are writing your own bass line, drum pattern or whatever'. Rick picks up the point: 'The rules were too cloudy. In the early days we didn't realise how important it was, and we let it go. But as soon as we'd done that with 'In The City' we'd set a precedent'.

'We've said this all along', continues Bruce, 'a lot of the tunes either stemmed from Rick's drum patterns or from me, as well as the times Paul came up with the original idea. On reflection we should have been given a small per- centage of the publishing, as much as a thankyou as any- thing else. Much later on we made a bit of a stand with getting a credit for 'Funeral Pyre', but a lot of the other songs which came about in exactly the same way are only credited to Paul'. As far as mistakes go, this was certainly

one of Rick and Bruce's costliest. 'But when you're eighteen
or whatever, you never think about the nitty gritty'.

Although Chris Parry was certainly 'sniffing around', the
band never really considered anyone aside from John
Weller to be a serious candidate for management. 'There
was only really one idea on which the whole band operated; to get more work. And John was really dedicated, his
efforts surpassed anyone's expectations. He was very
young at heart, and he became completely involved in the
whole thing. There wasn't really an occasion when he came
down on Paul's side unfairly'. In addition, he would not
feign expertise in an alien subject. Whether it be accoun-
tancy or legal matters, he would immediately seek advice
from an informed source. Despite his trusting nature, his
level-headed approach contributed significantly to the
band's progress.

However, Chris Parry's role was more important than
merely a conduit to a major record company. The band
remember several occasions when his 'big fat expenses
account' came in useful for subsistence. Taking a hand in
production, he was interested in both publishing and management. However, when it became obvious that The Jam
came as a self-contained package, he would look elsewhere.
'He probably thought we were promising, but just up from
the country and a bit green. I don't think he wanted to take
advantage of us, but he was very career minded and obviously saw in us a way to make his mark'.

Parry also brought along his friend, and fellow Polydor
employee, Vic Smith (later Vic Coppersmith Heaven) to see
the band at the Half Moon in Putney. As convinced as
Parry of the group's potential, he agreed to share production duties. 'I seem to remember it being a case of Vic being
brought in to support Chris in the early stages,' recalls
Rick. 'His main claim to fame was being the man who

turned the record button on when 'Honky Tonk Woman' was being played by the Rolling Stones. Apparently the producer was actually standing behind Charlie Watts playing the cowbell at the beginning.' He was also resident at Decca when the Beatles failed their audition.

In May 1977 the band joined up with the Clash's White Riot tour, which seemed to represent an ideal opportunity to raise their profile. However, only a handful of dates were completed. Pieced together in a hurry, the whole affair was shoddily planned. Although the musicians involved mixed quite happily, there was some antagonism between the band and Clash manager Bernard Rhodes.

Rhodes wanted the signed bands (i.e. the Clash and Jam) to subsidise the other acts; Buzzcocks, Slits, and Subway Sect. However, with The Jam having to pay for the use of the Clash PA, and 'buy' their way on to the tour, John Weller decided there was too much money coming out of his pocket. Particularly as they were only getting second billing. Apart from anything else, Rhodes was also the manager of Subway Sect. 'We were dismayed by the fact that the ideals of the punk movement had been so quickly diluted. There were all these petty arguments over lighting and billing, and the PA's were too small and things. It was a bit disillusioning and not at all what this punk thing was cracked up to be'.

The Rainbow gig proved the final straw. Unable to sound check, The Jam's sound was awful, and there were rumours that this may have been caused by deliberate tampering. The Jam took the decision to pull out of the tour with eight dates to play. A decision was quickly taken to sort out a tour on their own terms, now that their fan base had swelled sufficiently to accommodate this.

The eye-opening Clash debacle at least offered some comic

THE JAM
REQUIRE
KEYBOARD / VOCALS
Age 17-20 Clean image
Early Tamala, Atlantic R&B style
Telephone: Woking ▓▓▓▓ - Byfleet ▓▓▓▓

The Jam
ROCK & ROLL GROUP
Woking ☎ ▓▓▓▓

Paul Weller
Rhythm

Bruce Foxton
Bass Guitar

Steve Brooks
Lead Guitar

Rick Buckler
Drums

ONE OF THE LAST SHOWS AT MICHAEL'S CLUB
STEVE BROOKES, BRUCE (ON RHYTHM!!??) AND PAUL
CHECK OUT THE HAIR, FLARES AND SHOES

THE RED COW

BACKSTAGE & HAPPY AFTER A SUCCESSFUL EARLY GIG

THE JAM IS FORMED!

52

RAISING FUNDS FOR THE YMCA WOKING 1980.
BACK TO OUR ROOTS

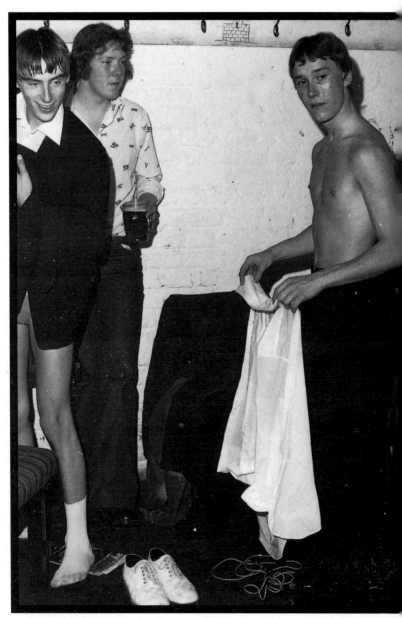

54

WE FOUND A BRITISH PUB IN LA
HAD TO SHARE A PINT THOUGH

THE LONSDALE YEARS

WAITING TO GO ON STAGE AT THE 100 CLUB - OXFORD
STREET, 1976

THE FIRST GIG AT THE FAMOUS 'MARQUEE'

WHERE'S THAT HELICOPTER?

CLASSIC EARLY SET

JAM/CLASH INTER-NEW WAVE FEUDING

Friendly faces from the New Wave . . . Right: Strummer of The Clash; and left, Paul Weller of The Jam

THE CLASH and The Jam on the same tour looked great on paper, especially with the front-runners being joined on the road with those great white hopes the all-girl band Slits. The Subway Sect and, the toast of the north, the very fine Buzzcocks.

It it had succeeded then the internal feuding on the initial part of the Anarchy tour — that led to The Damned quitting the tour — could have possibly been remembered as merely growing pains in a movement that had yet to learn one simple fact — if the bureaucrats in Remote Control divide the New Wave then they sure as hell will crush (or at the very least tame) the same movement. Every day new councils ban young bands from playing in their towns without valid reasons.

But The Jam left the tour after the Rainbow gig with eight dates still to play, and I couldn't help wondering if maybe we were doing the job for them . . . .

So — why didn't The Jam stay on the road with The Clash? Both sides see it very differently.

Clash manager Bernard Rhodes says that the fundamental idea behind the tour was that The Jam and The Clash were the only two bands signed with a record company, and that they had a responsibility to financially help the other bands on the bill.

"Chris Parry of Polydor and The Jam are only concerned about themselves," Bernie claims. "The Clash believe that the bigger bands have a duty to help out the bands that aren't signed to a record company — help them with money, use of lights and PA, anything you can. The Jam didn't want to know, and as for them saying that they had to pay to get on the tour, that's definitely not true. We haven't got a penny from them, and as a matter of fact they were getting one

was unavailable for a soundcheck before both the Rainbow and Edinburgh gigs.

"We were promised the use of the PA and we didn't always get it," said Paul Weller.

"On stage at the Rainbow the sound was so bad that I couldn't even hear myself, and it ruined the set," claimed bass player Bruce Foxton.

Of the actual financial details the band said they'd been asked to pay some money for appearing on the tour, and said they'd been willing to help the other bands to a certain degree — but they claim that the amount of money they were eventually being asked to contribute was more than they thought was worthwhile.

"Being asked to put our hands in our pockets all the time, was how it became," John Weller, Paul's Dad and manager of The Jam, told me.

"It was the same old story," said Polydor press officer Jeff Dcne. "Our A&R men have informed me that the money we were being asked to pay for appearing on the tour became too much."

How much?

"I believe somewhere in the region of a thousand pounds," Bernie Rhodes said they haven't received a penny from Polydor or The Jam.

"In fact no money has actually changed hands," Jeff agreed.

He expressed the same sentiments as The Jam about being promised full use of lights and PA and then not being given them. As well as pointing out that The Jam had already been the victims of narrow-minded local council bureaucracy on their own headlining tour.

"The City Council in Leeds have already banned The Jam from appearing at the Leeds Town Hall," said Jeff. And the list gets longer everyday

— see page 3.

And while we fight amongst ourselves, can you hear the real enemy laughing? □ TONY PARSONS

hundred quid each night to play a gig. They didn't give us a penny and they had use of our lights, PA, backdrop, the lot.

"Chris Parry has claimed we demanded a four-figure sum from The Jam but we haven't got a penny out of them and we've lost 17,000 quid on this tour subsidising the smaller bands. But all Chris Parry and The Jam care about is themselves . . ."

The friction with The Jam is certainly not the only aggravation the tour has encountered. Subway Sect's drummer has left to replace John Towes in Generation X, and after the gig in St. Albans the bands on the coach were all taken down the local police station by The Law.

"We were all stripped bollock-naked," Bernie says. "Fingers up the anus, the works."

What about The Jam's and Polydor's argument that friction was caused by you managing The Subway Sect as well as The Clash?

"I don't manage The Subway Sect!" he explodes. "I am not the manager of The Subway Sect! Look, we just care about bands other than ourselves and we're concerned about putting on a great show for the kids . . . So you're out on the road keeping things together?

"Yeah," Bernie says. "And while I'm out here CBS release 'Remote Control' as a single. That's very ironic."

Anything to add on the split between The Clash and The Jam?

"I don't give a shit about Chris Parry or The Jam," he concludes.

When I spoke to the members of The Jam last week they said that the split had occured because the PA that they had been promised the use of

HEADLINED AGAIN

58

POST OFFICE

TELEGRAM

Prefix. Time handed in.   Office of origin and Service Instructions.   Words.

No. _____

OFFICE STAMP

rges to pay

Tariff £
V.A.T. £
Total £

RECEIVED

From _____ 72

By _____

At _____ m
To _____
By _____

K 79 2228 ABERDEEN EH 29

OVERNIGHT THE JAM PLAYHOUSE EDINBURGH =

CONGRATULATIONS ON VICTORY ON MERSYSIDE AND MANCHESTER

. MAGGIE WILL BE PROUD OF YOU SEE YOU IN SOUTHAFRICA

FOR GUN PRACTWCE . =   THE CLASH

THE JAM GW 721

B or C

For free repetition of doubtful words telephone "TELEGRAMS ENQUIRY" or call, with this form
at office of delivery. Other enquiries should be accompanied by this form, and, if possible, the envelope.

56-1390 8/74 K & F

GW721 K79

POST OFFICE
OVERNIGHT TELEGRAM

THE JAM
PLAYHOUSE
EDINBURGH

THE TELEGRAM FROM THE CLASH

FIRST THE EYE, NOW THE LEG

"C'MON RICK, LETS GET A BEER, I'VE HAD A BAD DAY"

CLASSIC JAM

HOW DO I GET OUT OF HERE?

THOSE INJECTIONS HURT DON'T THEY?

RACE YOU TO THE FRONT OF THE STAGE

moments. At the same Rainbow gig, security had decided to disrobe the audience of anything that could be construed as being a weapon. Punk fashion of the time incorporated ammunition belts, motorcycle boots and studs, all of which had to be left behind outside the auditorium. Hence many viewers had to pogo their way through the night in their socks, and, in Rick's words: 'The Rainbow's foyer looked like a ten-foot high, third world munitions' dump'.

The energy of the new wave also brought about another change in venue policy. 'Most concert halls had been converted from cinemas, and were decked out with rows of seating or chairs. At the punk gigs audiences just started smashing it into firewood. Several times our road crew and audience had to try to create a bit of room down the front by passing all this broken wood back over their heads'. The venues quickly cottoned on that they could actually charge an extra fee for removing seating before a gig, and replacing it afterwards. Even, as Rick notes, 'if it would have to be replaced anyway for the following evening, when they could charge the next act a fee for installing it'. Such practices occasionally continue to this day.

Playing gigs in the capital was one obvious way of drawing attention to the band. Another was to say something controversial. Weller took it upon himself to make his famous statement about voting Conservative at the next general election in the Jam's first major music press interview. If his intention was to wind up the media's pseudo-liberals, it achieved this and more. The Clash appreciated it so much they sent the band a sarcastic telegram. The effect was compounded when The Jam played under the 'Jubilee' heading. Although primarily intended to embrace audiences who weren't able to attend the major venues in London, these three gigs (Chelsea, Tower Hamlets and Battersea) nevertheless flew in the face of the Pistols' 'God Save The Queen' sentiments. 'For us, the key element to these gigs was that they were free to enter'. Despite appearances, the band were neither particularly pro nor anti-monarchy. But the spectre of Paul's approving comments on Elizabeth II and the Conservative Party would take a long time to shake off.

The Jam made their recorded debut with 'In The City' in April 1977. The most stylish of their early material, it was a rousing song which neatly married the romance and vulnerability of youthful expectation. On the back of the band's growing live reputation it reached a healthy number 40 in the nation's charts. The previously cautious parents of Rick and Bruce saw their patience rewarded with approving comments from neighbours when the band appeared on 'Top Of The Pops' in May 1977. "Ooh, Mrs Buckler, saw your lad on the telly last night, he's done really well for himself". 'In The City' also brought a significant nod from a less likely source. Steve Jones, that celebrated tea-leaf, proceeded to half-inch the riff for the Sex Pistols 'Holidays In The Sun'.

If the band's first album , recorded over just eleven days, confirmed anything, it was the huge potential of Polydor's investment. Covers of Larry Williams' 'Slowdown' and 'The Batman Theme' which closed their encores in the early days (it was also recorded, of course, by the Who) suggested that their nascent English charm would be better served by more time and space. 'We basically just recorded it live, banged it straight out, without any overdubs'. Weller's lyrics are simplistic in retrospect, heartfelt sloganeering but rhetoric nevertheless. The album was basically a document of their live set, but about a third of the tracks rise above a robust energy. The title-track and 'Away From The Numbers' (Weller's first statement of identity and intent) were the two stand-outs. 'Non-stop Dancing' was an adequate tribute to Northern Soul all-nighters, while 'I Got By In Time' delivered the first of Weller's proclamations of fallibility: 'I didn't mean to fail anyone, but you know its something that I do'. Such prose, if not the sentiments, are straight out of the 60s. 'It was all done really quickly, but the sessions felt really good. We really felt things were happening'. 'In The City' stands alongside the debuts of the Sex Pistols, Clash, Banshees, Stranglers and Damned as a definitive, exciting snapshot of the period. Accordingly, the first album was attacked for being too plagiaristic of the Who's 'My Generation'. It certainly featured its fair share of chord progressions in the Townshend mould.

Sixty copies of the LP were signed by the band and given away to selected writers and DJs. This in an age when any form of self-promotion was frowned upon, at least in public. It demonstrated once more The Jam's earnest desire to break out of the punk ghetto. Their neat attire also helped bring them in to sharp relief against the rest of the London in-crowd. Their 'mod' image was somewhat over-played by the media. All three members pointed out at some length that prior to punk there was no other youth movement they could share any common ground with. Paul and Bruce in particular embraced the working class traditions of looking sharp and clean cut, unlike the Clash's shabby military attire. Whilst being senior players in the punk vanguard, this also helped stir a revival of the 'Mod' culture.

'We kept getting asked by journalists', recalls Rick, 'whether or not we would call ourselves a punk band. "Well, no, not really", we would say. So then they would ask if we were a Mod band. And we would say, "Well, no we're not, not really". And it carried on like that all through our career'.

The reaction of the media was generally favourable, aside from those who hadn't forgiven Paul's political leanings. 'The Jam certainly have it in them to do great things but somebody's trying to get too much out of it much too soon'

The JAM

was the theory advanced by the band's old friend Chas De Whalley. He probably wasn't that far short of the mark, though the next time Rick saw him he threw him into a cold bath for his troubles anyway.

It was also during the heady year of 1977 that the band experienced one of its few bust-ups. They had just played the Hope And Anchor in Islington, and were due to fly out to France the next day. They were still using low-key transport, and had this time been lumbered with a cluttered transit van. Trying to find some degree of comfort on a set of 4' x 4' planks, Bruce accidentally sat on the caseless Hoffner Violin Bass lent to him by Paul. It was a direct copy of Paul McCartney's version, only right-handed, and it meant a great deal to Paul despite the fact that he had long since transferred from four stringed duties. The neck was neatly snapped in two.

'Paul just went completely mad. I never got the chance to get an apology out before he started thumping me'. John and Ann Weller had made a lot of sacrifices a few years earlier in order to afford the instrument, and it was still close to Paul's heart. It was, however, an accident. John Weller came back to the van after finalising his management duties to find his son and Bruce immersed in a full-blown fist-fight. Rick, who was doing his best to stay out of the way of the flaying limbs, overheard him bemoan the fact that with the band just about to make it, two out of the three of them had decided to kill each other.

The gig in Paris the following day indicated that Paul had come out of the fracas slightly the better: 'If you look at any pictures of that night, you'll notice what a corking black eye I've got'.

Another early benchmark was hearing 'In The City' played on the jukebox of their drinking den, the Prince of Wales in

The JAM

Maybury. None of the band were the sort to charge around hoisting barmaids in the air and kissing babies, but the song's presence next to other hits of the day and the old standards brought quiet satisfaction.

After the disastrous Clash affair, they also set about organising their own UK tour proper. Running from June 4 to July 24 it began in Birmingham, and was due to span 40 dates, but had to be cut short. The band have strong memories of sitting in the Holiday Inn for the first time puzzling over exactly what they should do in their hotel rooms. 'OK, we're here, four hours to the gig, what do we do now? Are we pop stars now and how do pop stars behave anyway. Should we throw the TV set out the window or what?' They soon acclimatised however, and sleeping in a different town every night would become second nature. It would not be long before Rick had perfected the technique of taking a box of hotel matches with him so that if he got lost he would know what town he was supposed to be in, and where he should be sleeping that night.

Such early ventures were marked by a grand economy of scale. Booking the cheapest hotels on the route brought them face to face with the real rock 'n' roll lifestyle; stodgy little B&B's with no facilities worth talking about. The final straw came in Sheffield when Rick and Bruce were sharing a room ('As if actually sharing a room with each other wasn't bad enough'). Equipped with a rudimentary fold-out shower contraption in the corner, Bruce was forced to give up any pretensions to hygiene when it collapsed for the final time. His attempts at origami were comprehensively defeated by his opponent, though he made enough noise in the process to wake the entire hotel. 'That was it. We decided that we'd have to go just a little more upmarket in future'.

His inability to cope with the unit won him the nickname

The JAM

'Shower Curtain' amongst the roadies. Paul, meanwhile, with his propensity for carrying vast amounts of cigarettes, paper and accumulated detritus in his inflated jacket pockets, became 'Saddlebags'.

Rick had moved on from being called 'Pube', a titled coined for no apparent reason, or none that anyone will admit. Now, due to the customary dark glasses he wore on stage, his new moniker was 'Blind Boy'. Which had nothing to do, as one journalist concluded, with any over indulgence in self expression which purportedly results in the condition.

The physical rigour of this first tour definitely took its toll. 'It was completely over ambitious really, we had no idea how much hard work we were letting ourselves in for'. By its end the band were simply going through the motions, desperate to get back home. Their first show in Glasgow was a good example. The Scottish city had long been notorious for the fervour with which it greeted visiting musicians, and this night was no exception. Unfortunately for Paul, the steaming heat in the venue kept causing his Rickenbacker to go out of tune. Condensation was literally dripping from the ceiling. 'He just got so frustrated he started banging his head against the wall. Really hard too'.

Gigs at the Marquee are remembered with particular fondness. 'We always seemed to manage to arrive too late to do a sound check', remembers Rick. 'And we would begin our performances by loading our equipment over the heads of the audience on to the stage, and repeat the process to retrieve our instruments at the end of the night'.

Early on they played at High Wycombe with the Boys offering support. Paul found himself in an argument with 'Kid' Reid, the Boys' diminutive bass player. 'I can't remember why, but Paul had decided he was pissed off with this guy. He decided to resolve the situation by smashing a bottle and bashing him with it. Or at least he would have done had he been able to break the bottle'. Despite several, increasingly desperate efforts, the object remained defiantly intact. Cracked repeatedly against a table, it held out for so long that by the time it finally gave way, leaving only the neck, its handler had all but forgotten what the argument was about. Seeing as everyone else in the dressing room had collapsed in hysteria, a violent confrontation seemed somewhat unwarranted now.

By the time the band arrived at the Hammersmith Odeon for the last date of the tour, they had dispensed with their Union Jack backdrop. The rise of the National Front rendered its display a little precarious. Additionally, the overtones of violence and tension were running high throughout a year given over to rabid media patriotism.

The early gigs caught the spirit of the punk phenomenon perfectly. However much they distanced themselves from the more blinkered philosophies extolled by many, The Jam represented one of the most authentic adrenaline buzzes on the circuit. The spectre of violence, much exaggerated by the media for its own purposes, crept in only occasionally. A gig at Hastings in 1977 saw massive fights in the audience, as provincial towns sought to imitate what they perceived was happening in London. 'It was never actually that violent in London. But when you got out to the provinces all these people really believed that punk was just like the media portrayed it'. The chaos of the night was recorded by photographer Walt Davidson, though his film was confiscated by the authorities. 'They didn't want that sort of thing associated with their town', remembers Bruce.

Despite being one of the most professional bands to emerge as part of the punk axis, The Jam were not averse to a spirit of adventure. 'One of those early tours we ended up in Bristol, and we decided that the 'rider' should be consumed on stage. The plan being that the entire lot should be quaffed before we left the audience'. Not surprisingly, no-one seems to remember whether or not this was achieved, but by the end of the performance, with the stage looking like a burgled off-licence, the protagonists were barely capable of finding the stage door, never mind perform an encore.

Vic Coppersmith Heaven had followed Chris Parry's lead by familiarising himself not just with The Jam's studio world, but their demeanour on stage. Popular with the band for his sympathetic and knowledgeable input, he became an ardent supporter of the cause. Of course, this made him fair game for laddish pranks. Playing the Paradiso in Holland, the producer came out to see his pro-tégés. As was his manner, he arrived bedecked in one of the flowery, lurid shirts his wife liked to design for him. Back in his hotel room, this very garment had caught the atten-tion of Rick: 'I thought it looked a bit 'girlie' basically. So I thought I'd set fire to it'. Unfortunately for Vic, he was still wearing it at the time. From then on any description of Coppersmith Heaven's work as a 'hot producer' was guar-anteed to produce a few wry smiles in The Jam camp.

The only real 'competition' within the gaggle of new bands concerned the release of the first 'punk single'. The Damned's 'New Rose' beat several other acts to the punch. Otherwise, The Jam took their place alongside their peers with solidarity and enthusiasm. The Sex Pistols' violent upsurge left space for new bands, new fanzine writers and journalists, and the spirit of the times was one of conquest rather than division. Even so, there were justified suspi-cions about several groups who really were too old, or too privileged, to be singing about teenage life in council flats.

It wasn't until an early date in Amsterdam, for instance, that Rick Buckler first caught sight of label-mates Siouxsie

2

& The Banshees. His summary: 'They were absolutely awful'. And Paul did manage to enter into a slight altercation with Sid Vicious concerning developments within the punk elite at the Speakeasy (the preferred London drinking hole of the times). Surprisingly, perhaps, Vicious came off worse. Paul smashed a bottle in his face, before making a smart exit. Vicious' delicate features were never quite the same again. In the months that followed there was considerable paranoia about the Pistols and their fans being out to 'get The Jam'.

There was a small run-in too with their madcap punk brethren, the Damned. When The Jam's debut long-player arrived, they took the trouble to ring Stiff's offices, to trade it for the recently released 'Damned Damned Damned'. 'We heard through the grapevine that the Damned might be devising some devilish stunt to play on us. Because we knew what their reputation was, we decided we shouldn't be outdone. So we took a copy of our album into the toilet, shat in it, and sealed it up in a parcel'.

The Damned package arrived a few days later. With great trepidation, they poked away at its casing, until the foul item was eventually revealed. A copy of the Damned's debut platter smeared in jam. 'Not very original really, just a gentle little rib-tickler. We were expecting something much more outrageous'. Meanwhile, The Jam's own package, which had sat in an out-tray ripening for a few days, was winging its way across London....

Toilet humour played no small part in The Jam's career. It is a little known fact that Paul Weller actually suffered from toilet seat phobia. He simply could not manage his number two's unless he had carefully spread tissue paper on top of the receptacle first. And this would probably have remained a secret for all time had he not walked out of the gent's one day trailing three yards of toilet paper behind him, tucked in to his trousers. 'Well', concludes Bruce, 'he couldn't really deny it then, could he?'

The depravity did not end there. A favourite trick from those first tours was to leave a 'chocolate log' in the unwitting recipient's bath. They were impossible to flush or remove in any way that did not expose the victim to a rather grisly process of disposal. Many times showers had to be taken with feet placed securely wide of the offending item.

'Such is the lifestyle of the young rock 'n' roller' sighs Rick.

CHAPTER THREE

All That Rugby Puts Hairs
On Your Chest

Having acquainted themselves with the domestic circuit, foreign conquest was next on the cards. France would always harbour a soft spot for the trio. On their first jaunt there on August 6, 1977, for the Mont De Marson Festival, the band found themselves in trouble for attempting to play, drunkenly, in the fountain. Once more the Damned were in the vicinity, and while Paul and Bruce were escorted away for their illicit behaviour, Rick returned from the supermarket with the latest in DIY hair-dying kits. Applied immediately, and with disastrous effect, the black hands and black streaks adorning his bonce did little to dispel the local gendarme's concerns about the 'nasty punk rockers' infesting their town. John Weller, meanwhile, struggled to convince the authorities of his charges' innocence in a foreign language. 'It was a bit of a panic moment', recalls Bruce, 'but watching John trying to speak Franglaise to these policemen topped it off really. We couldn't stop laughing.'

Mont De Marson was advertised as the first major European punk Festival, with The Jam, Clash, and Damned playing on Saturday night. However, John Weller decided to pull out after learning that The Jam would be playing after the Clash, as he thought the audience might follow them home. The decision still seems strange in retrospect.

The Jam enjoyed more luck, however, than their heroes Dr Feelgood, who also appeared at Mont De Marson on a different night. Arriving on a separate flight, the pub rockers plane was hit halfway across the English Channel by a bolt of lightning. Luckily for them, it didn't 'earth' itself on the airliner, which managed to land despite a twisted nose.

Foreign visits were almost always guaranteed to generate problems at this early stage in their career. On another occasion in the same country they played outdoors for two or three numbers at a time before the generators packed in. 'The French technicians hadn't got their act together, and for a while a potential riot seemed to be in the offing'. Undoubtedly the worst case, however, was an abortive trip to Belgium, before they were signed. Convinced by a would-be promoter in England that the event would be laid on for them, they drove all the way to discover that no arrangements had been made for their accommodation. 'The promised hotel did not exist, and we were instructed that we could sleep on the stairs of the venue. A really excellent idea that'. In the event they decided to catch their beauty sleep in the car. The gig was a non-event, with a disinterested, alarmingly small audience, and equipment that would shame Sheerwater Youth Club. 'That was a fairly classic case of us being completely green and trusting this idiot when we should have known better, or checked him out'.

With Chris Parry's encouragement, the band found time for an exploratory stab at the States. Their first US tour took in some sixteen shows in just twelve days. Parry, for his sins, was left to sort out the visas and buy the plane fares on his credit card. Only first he had to get them there; both John and Paul Weller turned out to be absolutely terrified of flying.

To quell their nerves, they turned to the bottle. Which left Parry with the unenviable role of schoolteacher both on board and off. By the time the plane landed the situation had not improved. Paul was the worst for wear, having emptied most of the in-flight bar's contents to drown his nerves. Parry, a little more experienced at this global touring lark, knew the chances of any rock band walking through customs being stopped and thoroughly searched for several hours was high. 'The fact that Paul could hardly negotiate the customs channel was not about to help our chances'.

Paul stayed in his best truculent mood throughout the tour. At New York's CBGB's he told one journalist that he wasn't interested in looking round the Big Apple because he'd seen it all on television anyway - a quite magnificent arrogance. After their debut appearance at LA's Whiskey A Go Go, they postponed the subsequent Californian show at San Francisco's Old Wardolf. Chris Parry was not best pleased.

Paul and tour manager Dickie Bell had become, quite unreasonably, paranoid about the leakage from one of the amps. They decided the band might get electrocuted and they were not going to do the gig. Which left Parry with a great deal of explaining to do, having spent weeks pulling together dozens of record company moguls, producers, PR and press especially for the gig. Some of them had even flown in from the East Coast. Subsequently, there was little love lost between Parry and Bell, each of whom thought the other was trying to take over the band.

The tour had one other unsavoury, and unforeseen, effect; 'We only had one suit each'. Often playing two high energy sets in each town before moving on to the next city, by the time they arrived in New York their suits could very nearly have taken the stage of their own accord.

There were more of Paul's tantrums to endure before they could get home, however. At a specially conducted press conference, fending off admittedly silly questions about punk rock, Paul switched in to sullen, arrogant, 'You are stupid Americans' mode. Pushing Chris Parry further into apoplexy in the process.

After one of their better sets at CBGB's, Paul encouraged the audience to remove the seating. The temperature rose as the venue was trashed and Paul, on stage, announced that The Jam were splitting. Which just about killed Chris Parry, who had tried to make amends to his record company contacts by shipping them out to this gig instead, alongside members of Polydor UK who had specially flown in.

Afterwards they were too tired to greet their effervescent record company staff and management. They merely wanted to rush backstage and peel off their by now soaking garments. 'We felt a little bit guilty' recalls Rick, 'because they had obviously come over expecting a big back-slapping party. But we were just totally exhausted. It wasn't actually anything personal'. They did, however, bump into Jerry Ramone. Apparently sober, he came backstage, told the band how great they were, fell over backwards and passed out.

Bruce has mixed memories of pumping the flesh of America's 'no wave' generation. 'Patti Smith came back too, and some of the Blondie people. I think Patti walked straight out again when we didn't make a big fuss over her'.

It all seemed a bit strange to the Brits. As the cliché runs, everything in New York seemed larger than life. When publisher Brian Morrison arrived to take them to their first gig, and pulled up in a huge white limousine a street long,

The JAM

they decided it was time to call a taxi. Morrison, puffing on a cigar whose length rivalled that of the vehicle, was clearly bemused by such behaviour. The Jam's audiences were similarly non-plussed by the band's rough, doggedly English songbook. The response on this first voyage across the Atlantic was polite but cautious, the band's frustration becoming increasingly evident at successive shows.

One of the reasons Paul was so difficult on the trip was due to his recent liaison with a girl called Gill Price. For the first time in his young life Paul Weller was in love. Which was wonderful for him, but it nearly had disastrous results for The Jam. By the time the sessions for the second album began, Paul and Gill were sharing a flat in London's Baker Street.

July 1977 saw the arrival of the band's second single, 'All Around The World'. It had been recorded during a break in the first tour's itinerary, caused by the Damned playing at the venue a week before and wrecking the joint. The proprietors decided they didn't want to book any more of these punk acts for a while.

All Around The World' was premiered by a bizarre appearance on Marc Bolan's TV show. After several rehearsals, the band bolted their way through the song. All went well until the track's climax, at which point Rick lost one of his sticks in the air. 'Approximately three seconds later I realised that the stick was not going to come down'. Quite how it had managed to defy the laws of gravity were not immediately apparent, but the group felt sure they would be allowed to do a second take. 'Marc Bolan just stepped in front of the camera. God knows what they'd have done if we'd done it in the middle of the song, they'd have had to do it again, but because it was the end they just didn't bother'. Unfortunately, the technicians were working to a tight deadline, and The Jam's second major television appearance was committed to posterity with Rick Buckler looking helplessly skywards.

If the first album had been applauded in more quarters than not, the second provided the band with their first hitch. With the unexpected success of 'In The City', pressure was mounting from Polydor to exploit the commercial potential of the band. And it meant they got another £20,000 advance.

The second album started its life in bizarre fashion. Chris Parry had come up with the bright idea of sending them to a farmhouse in the middle of nowhere to give Paul's songwriting fresh inspiration. It had the opposite effect. Completely without distraction, Paul, Rick and Bruce merely spent their time in the local pub, which was about the only other feature on the landscape. The farmhouse was owned by Trevor Morantz . 'It was in the middle of nowhere, and we didn't have a car or any transport. To top it off, the farmhouse description was misleading too. It was *going* to be a farmhouse studio, but at that point in time it was just a portakabin and some derelict stables and a Dansette Major between us'. The band weren't even allowed in to the farmhouse itself as that was where the family lived.

'We had a go, but it just wasn't the right environment', adds Bruce, 'it was cut short because we were climbing the walls. What do you do, apart from sit in the rehearsal room - there's only so much jamming or whatever you can get through. We were supposed to be there to write, but we were just wasting time and money'. Although the excursion was meant to last a fortnight, it was mercifully cut down to a single week.

When 'All Around The World' charted, Chris Parry came down to share the good news, and check on progress to

The Jam

date. 'Which was another good excuse to go for a drink, I seem to remember'.

Eventually the band cut their losses and began work in Basing Street Studios, Notting Hill, in August 1977. However, the frustration did not end with a change of surroundings. Basing Street was a positively 'pokey' studio by modern standards, and Paul could not get his Rickenbackers in tune for the life of him. Although the faithful Rickenbacker undoubtedly suited Weller's sense of style, he might have tempered his original penchant for the guitar had he known how difficult it was to keep in tune. By the recording of The Jam's second album he was not beyond smashing one or two up when they proved particularly troublesome.

Just six short months after their debut they presented 'This Is The Modern World' to a nation, bedecked in a moody photograph, with the tower blocks of West Way London in the background. The pressure for Paul to write the album to order, with the record label trying to make hay while the sun shone, was soon apparent. Unlike their debut, the songs had not been thoroughly road tested and it showed. While critics bemoaned the inclusion of slower material, the use of first-time overdubs failed to mask the rushed nature of many of the songs. Chris Parry and Vic Coppersmith Heaven were again at the controls, and this time round the production was noticeably 'thin'.

The biggest problem remained the songwriting. 'Basically, Paul was far too busy being 'into' Gill than was healthy'. Bruce and Rick remember innumerable hold ups when they would have to wait for Paul to finish an overdub because he and Gill had decided to have sex in the rehearsal room. Again. On the first album angry and passionate, Paul was basically having far too good a time to deliver the goods on the second. And Bruce and Rick sensed he was losing interest in The Jam.

Paul's lack of conviction saw Bruce being given far more of the songwriting credits. While Bruce's songs were up to scratch musically, he didn't share Paul's lyrical scope and he became an easy target for the press. Rick's view of The Jam's much maligned second LP is a little more sympathetic: 'The second album was a bit more serious because obviously it was all written just to be recorded, and that was a complete change from the first LP. Even though it was slated at the time, looking back, I think its still just as good as any of the other albums, because it was a phase that we went through. It was always said that The Jam were signed too early and that maybe another year would have done us a lot of good in terms of the final recordings, but I don't really agree with that'.

'The Modern World' tour, covering November 17 to December 18, was less exhaustive, and many of the songs taken to task by the critics, improved for having been played in on the road. The dates spanned an appearance on the noted Northern TV show 'So It Goes', presented by Factory supremo Anthony Wilson. However, Paul was still, evidently, not a happy man. At the Derby date he threatened to walk off stage if the audience did not desist from spitting. Which was also a bugbear of Bruce's, especially the occasions when 'A big, horrible lump of phlegm would land and dangle off the end of your machine head. Knowing full well that sooner or later, especially playing the temperamental Rickenbacker, I would have to tune up...'

An even more terrible fate awaited The Jam's bass player after playing the Queen's Hall in Leeds. The band came back to their hotel, now known as the Hilton. Post-gig celebrations were muted by the fact that the bar had closed. Instead The Jam, their entourage, and the entire Australian rugby team who were also staying there, sought service from a small, dumb waiter service hatch. Which proved a considerable handicap to the usual after show inebriation which had become customary.

Paul, on finally retrieving a round of drinks, had them accidentally knocked over by an older gentleman in the queue. Which proved unfortunate for the miscreant, as Paul picked up a glass and lashed out at him. The result was a minor cut to the forehead. Even more unfortunate was Paul, however. The victim turned out to be the Australian rugby team's manager.

'It was a bit of an over the top reaction, he was obviously pissed off that his drinks had been spilt, but glassing anyone's face is out of order' notes Bruce.

Twenty two frighteningly huge rugby players promptly decided they wanted to kill anybody remotely connected with The Jam. The message had gone back that a bunch of limey punk rockers had bottled their head honcho, and they were out for blood. Bruce, Rick and Paul found themselves on a desperate chase through hotel corridors. 'All I can remember about that' winces Bruce 'is getting cornered. You know the archetypal long and narrow hotel corridors, and I couldn't find my room in the panic, and I was trapped. I don't know how many of these rugby players there were, it must have been ten to one. They kicked seven shades of shit out of me. I had cracked ribs, the lot, and was bandaged up for the rest of the tour'. Which seemed a little unjust for someone quite innocent in the whole affair.

Even when the police arrived, it seemed for one moment that they would be unable to protect the band. They were, after all, only half the size of the assembled rugby toughs. Unable to guarantee their safety, the Motorbike Police escorted the group in the early hours of the morning to another hotel, the Dragonara. It wasn't very salubrious, but it was safe. Paul was actually arrested for his part in the incident, spending the night in a police cell. He received a sizeable fine and was bound over to keep the peace. At his court appearance, some thoughtful Jam fans scrawled "Paul Weller is innocent" on the pavement outside. He wasn't.

It is generally accepted that the night's events were the reason The Jam never toured in Australia: Paul was convinced that as soon as he stepped off the plane his friends from the rugby team would be there waiting for him.

1978 began with two surprise appearances at the Marquee, followed by dates at the 100 Club and Music Machine. The gigs, covering February and March, came under the nom de plume 'The London Blitz', and acted as a warm-up for further foreign ventures.

The dates coincided with the release of the first single written by Bruce Foxton, 'News Of The World'. Reaching a healthy number 27 in the charts, it received short shrift from some critics. Musically it was as good as most of The Jam's early fare, but Bruce accepts its lyrical failings as 'fair comment'. Having recorded their first video for 'In The City' at one of Shepperton's huge sound stages, this time round The Jam went for something a little more dramatic. The plan was to film on top of Battersea Power Station, and hire a helicopter to film scenes over the capital. Which wasn't quite how it turned out: 'For a start they wouldn't let us get to the top of the Power Station, we couldn't get permission. Then the helicopter didn't turn up. We were all standing there waiting for it, staring up at the sky.' recalls Bruce. 'Then we found out it had been cancelled because of high winds, which didn't surprise us because we were nearly blown off the building ourselves'.

Turning their sights once more to the US, the band struck a

co-management deal for the States with Eric Gardner, whose roster included Blue Oyster Cult. The Jam were duly invited to support, way down the bill, on a strange first tour proper of the US in 1978, from March to April. Blue Oyster Cult were playing 20,000 seaters, huge venues that seemed cavernous to the young Brits. There were three road crews, and bands dropped in and out of the tour on a regular basis. Aside from the fact that the group really didn't know what was going on for days at a time, it was a match made in hell. Proudly bouncing around on stage in their tight suits playing fast punk music, they were greeted with studied indifference by practically every audience. No matter how many bands appeared on the bill, The Jam were always firmly stuck at the bottom.

'We couldn't keep up with some of this because we were travelling in completely different mode - I think we were on donkeys or something - we couldn't keep up with it at all. It really didn't work cos you can imagine the sort of music that those bands were playing, and we'd go on there with our suits and play this sort of punk stuff at them. It just went right over their heads.'

In truth the tour was one of John Weller's most significant managerial mistakes. Rather than spending years converting small club audiences, which would have required him to coax Paul out of his anti-American sentiments, The Jam's manager had elected to try a short-cut into the heart of the beast. 'It was a disaster', offers Bruce, succinctly. Ironically, if John Weller had hoped to outflank his son's distrust of touring the States, he had only served to aggravate it. 'I think Paul was the most reluctant out of all of us to do these sort of tours abroad anyway, it was like putting more coal on the fire for him. He was saying "Well, I told you so, look at this one, this is a classic fucking balls up"'.

Glimpses of a silver lining were few and far between. When

they hooked up for a few dates with Be Bop Deluxe, they spotted a few locals at a date in Phoenix Arizona trying to incorporate what they had read was taking place in Britain. Hence token efforts at the pogo which left the all seated audiences even more mystified. The only other date to see any reaction on the same tour came when the band played on a revolving stage. As they looked up they saw a solitary young man dancing happily to the music. He was very quickly instructed to calm down. 'It was that sort of tour'.

'Taking the short cut from small clubs to stadia had back-fired, we just hadn't built a strong enough following in the States'. One particularly numbing baseball stadium crowd, 15,000 of them, booing in unison to The Jam's set, is just one of the memories to treasure from the tour. 'That,' observes Bruce, 'did absolute wonders for our self-confidence'.

Equally extraordinary were the promotional activities foisted on the band, a round of interviews conducted by radio stations unable to place them in any sort of context. One female DJ on the West Coast went so far as to demand a litre bottle of wine before consenting to interview them. Overhearing the argument in the foyer, the band elected to make their exit back to the hotel with a stiff 'We weren't having any of that nonsense' rebuke.

Breaking the US, the mythologised stamp of approval for British bands since the 60s beat boom, would grow to be a source of frustration for those involved with The Jam. They were a thousand miles, both physically and metaphorically, from Woking Working Men's Club.

John Weller discovered what he might have thought was 'home from home' on one of the first sorties to America; a downtown drinking club. Such establishments are notorious for their dim, atmospheric lighting. Walking up to the

The Jam

bar he nearly sat straight on the lap of a black guy enjoying his drink. 'Oh sorry', he exclaimed, 'I didn't see you sitting there', thereby adding insult to injury.

If Weller's disapproval of his Atlantic cousins is well recorded, the rest of The Jam were less than enamoured either: 'London was completely different. London had always gone through changes, with pub rock, moving onto punk. I think it still does have that sort of feel about it, its always been a fairly experimental city for that sort of thing. The Americans just really struck us as being a bit stagnant. Whereas we, and the British audiences, we'd really had enough of the Bee Gees.'

CHAPTER FOUR

A Distant Echo

The pace of The Jam's charge had been impressive, but had taken its toll. The summer of 1978 brought their first big setbacks. Exhaustion from two rushed albums and major tours nearly brought about a premature death. Paul hatched plans to open a second hand clothes store while Bruce drunkenly mused on the possibilities of running a seaside hotel ala Basil Fawlty. At least that was what was recorded by a 'Sounds' journalist when Bruce was drunk and thought he was speaking off the record: 'Yeh, the classic mistake. Never trust a journalist when he says he's on a night off'.

This turn of events had been brought about by Weller's writers block. It wasn't so much that he couldn't write songs, more that he couldn't write anything that wasn't a 'pile of shit'. Chris Parry was the man brave enough to inform him of this fact. The unreleased 'On Sunday Morning' reflected Weller's disillusionment in 1978, which had been severely aggravated by the US tour. He remembers this period as being one of personal reclusiveness with Gill. Also gone, perhaps forever, is 'I Want To Paint'. Like 'Tonight At Noon' from the previous album, it took its title from an Adrian Henri poem.

The Jam

Of the songs ditched from the scrapped third album, only 'Billy Hunt' and 'A Bomb In Waldour Street' would be transformed or accommodated for the third LP. Another rejection, Foxton's 'The Night', would surface on the b-side to 'Tube Station'.

The truth of the matter for those involved on the inside of The Jam was that Paul was so besotted in his affections for Gill that his songwriting had fallen by the wayside. No-one begrudged Paul his happiness, and both Rick and Bruce are keen to point out that they wouldn't want any band member interfering with their personal lives. However, his tempestuous relationship was having a seriously detrimental affect on his writing.

It is to Paul's credit that he rectified these problems for himself. Pulling himself clear of the romantic stupor which had overtaken him, he decided it was time to return home to his parents in Woking. It was an obvious effort to touch base with those things which had made him, and also to escape from the madness of the capital.

There was another advantage in getting out of London, above and beyond the obvious desire for a slacker pace and more relaxed atmosphere. Paul was being stalked by what might most kindly be termed a 'weirdo'. In a tale typical of fan adulation gone astray, a man insisted on lurking in the shadows outside Paul's flat. Not that he actually did anything, but his mere presence would see Paul skulking around in his own home, or getting dropped off on an adjacent street and entering the house from the rear.

This was the only real occasion on which fandom surpassed mere enthusiasm. Probably because The Jam were always so keen to talk to their audience, the gap between performer and fan was never allowed to grow so large that it could become a holding space for the psychological prob-

lems associated with obsession. The nearest Rick or Bruce
would come to such problems was the awe-struck devotee
in the dressing room, who simply could not bring themselves to say hello. 'I actually hated that', nods Bruce, 'those
silent types could be really disturbing. It was like you
weren't just two human beings talking to each other any
more, and I thought that was unhealthy.'

With the poor sales and ambivalent critical reaction to their
second album ringing in their ears, the pressure was building on everyone involved with The Jam. However, both
Rick and Bruce concede that the onus was much more on
Paul than themselves. He had to come up with decent
songs. Since leaving London he had written some new
material. Although still highly involved with Gill, their
relationship had at last passed the stage where every
second moment would involve sexual activity.

Following a short 'Seaside Tour' of the South Coast of
England, the band played Bilsen Festival in Belgium. It was
one of those occasions when Rick Buckler decided to cut
loose in the hotel. 'Well, it was fairly stupid really. I took
the fire hose off the corridor wall, and, using a copy of the
room layout from the tour itinerary, systematically opened
each door to Paul, Bruce, and the road crew's rooms, and
let them have it. Then I would duck straight back out
before they could see who it was. By the time someone had
called the police, I was safely tucked up in my bed. Silly
thing to do really, but its just another way of releasing pent
up energy during touring'.

On June the 18th the band were invited to appear on
Mickie Most's new television series 'Revolver'. John Weller
took the opportunity to seek out the teen hit-maker's
advice. Of the songs presented to him, Most suggested that
the band's chirpy cover version of the Ray Davies obscurity
'David Watts' was the most likely to dent the charts. Facing

stern critical judgement at home, the band elected to push it out as a single to give themselves some breathing space. If they were guilty of 'too many Little Englandisms', as Jon Savage records in 'England's Dreaming', this was all fuel to the fire. However, despite a modest chart return the single saw the band play 'Top Of The Pops' three times. Which caused Bruce a palpitation or two: 'I remember being on holiday down in Newquay with my mates and I had to phone up to get the chart positions. You had to phone up on a Tuesday morning in those days. And they said "Its at whatever, and you're doing Top Of The Pops". And so I had to leave my mates to get the overnight train back up to Paddington, and then get a bus to the BBC. And the conductor on the bus said, "Where to mate?". So I said "Take me to'Top Of The Pops'please".

So we had a laugh, and then the bus dropped me off a few yards from the BBC entrance on Wood Lane. And I walked through security and everyone else was arriving in limousines and record company cars. And here was I on the number 47 bus... So we recorded'Top Of The Pops'on Wednesday, and I came back to Woking to see my mum and dad, then got the train back to Newquay, and was back in the guest house Thursday evening - in time for Top Of The Pops! All the other guests were sat there watching the telly, and looking back at me. And of course, in those days people didn't really know it wasn't live, and they were saying "That's you!" - So I said, yeah, - "But you're here!". I think it took some of the older residents a while to come to terms with that'.

Paul, however, seemed determined not to enjoy the 'Top Of The Pops' experience, and went out of his way to mime badly. 'Alright, everyone knows how terrible it is, but it is a good way of getting your face on the telly and letting Joe Public hear your song. You're not going to look that credible, perhaps, but people do watch it'.

The JAM

The relative success of 'David Watts' spearheaded the band on to a ground-breaking appearance at the previously heavy-metal dominated Reading Festival. Unfortunately, the sound was terrible, and there was considerable hostility among the more traditional and conservative audience members.

'Down In The Tube Station At Midnight' was not merely a return to form but The Jam's first classic pop song. Previous singles, for all their laudable teen verve, had never really hinted that The Jam were capable of work like this. However, its release was somewhat arbitrary: 'After we'd recorded 'All Mod Cons' we felt really good about the album, and we thought just about everything on it could have been a single. Apart from 'Tube Station.' So, being as contrary as ever, that was the track The Jam decided should receive 7" billing.

It was the first time they had truly seized the unique opportunities offered by being a three piece. Foxton's fluent, busy bass line carries the whole song with sparse guitar hardly daring to interrupt for two thirds of its length. Full of sideways glances, the lyric measures absurdity against Weller's clever personification of the victim's outright terror. The hapless man's life flashes before his eyes, but his last thought is not of his wife, or indeed, of himself. His take away curry is getting cold on the floor. It is songwriting straight out of the Ray Davies school.

It would easily have breached the Top 10 had it not been for a quasi-ban imposed by the BBC. They found the subject matter disturbing, demonstrating once again powers of reasoning more befitting of pond life. Right down to the forboding cover picture, of Bond Street Tube Station, the single was a near perfect achievement.
Performing the song live did not always prove straightfor-

ward. By 1979 it was being used to open the set. Its underground echo motif, so vital in setting the tone of the single, was recorded as a regular intro. Unfortunately for one show the tape was lost, and panic ensued as to how they would emulate the sound. The solution was seemingly simple, purchase a copy of the record and use that. However, that particular night there was a time delay before the monitors kicked in. The five second gap allowed the first bars of the record to seep in, while The Jam stood on stage looking very much like poor mime artists. The song was stopped and the group started it on their own, amid considerable embarrassment.

Despite 'Tube Station's relative success, the third album would still be a make or break effort, with Polydor breathing down the band's necks for more hit singles. 'Our career up to then was sort of 1:1' muses Rick, 'going into extra time or penalties'. For the first time there was a real emphasis placed on the band to move in to a commercial direction. Thus they were forced to walk the thin line between more considered writing and the spontaneity that had been so evident on their debut.

The expectation for a Jam long player was made significantly more tangible by the success of the previous two singles. Soon after 'David Watts', sessions for the third album had got under way at RAK studios (rewarding Most for his help in selecting that track as a single). Chris Parry was politely informed that his services were no longer required.

Perhaps this had something to do with his dismissal of the earlier, abandoned, third album. Egos throughout the band had unquestionably been trod upon, even if individuals could accept that he was right. 'To all intents and purposes it was more a case of too many cooks - We got on alright with Vic and, anyway, we were beginning to learn more about what we were doing in the studio. It just seemed unnecessary to have a fifth person in tow'.

Parry retired from the scene with grace, but not until he had negotiated an advantageous share of the royalties for the work he had already done on 'All Mod Cons'. The break, though not without some regret on either side, proved that The Jam were growing as a band and taking greater control of their own destiny. The subsequent success of his Fiction label confirms the integrity of Parry's business sense, while his sponsorship of The Jam had already proved the quality of his ear.

'All Mod Cons' duly became The Jam's first great LP, showing up the bitterfest of the earlier brace for the launching pad that they were. The inner sleeve pictured several artefacts which were important to the band's development: A ska album, Union Jack badge, Motown single, rectangular shades etc. This conglomeration of influences was better realised than on any other recording. It also opened up a new wave of Mod fashion with Parkas and Ben Shermans sprouting from wardrobes the country over. A brief, media inflated Mod revival followed with groups like Secret Affair and The Chords. Unfortunately, the vast majority of bands who hung on to The Jam's coat tails were dull and inconsequential, which stripped the movement of any real platform.

For the first time there is a depth to Weller's lyrics which make a second reading essential. 'To Be Someone (Didn't We Have A Nice Time)' follows through on 'Away From The Numbers' by logging Weller's own progress to date. Just as fame and fortune have become attainable, these rewards are quickly diminished. 'A Bomb In Waldour Street' documented Weller's disenchantment with the development of the punk scene, particularly after an evening of negative vibes down at the Vortex. Elsewhere

'Billy Hunt' is a classy slice of school yard revenge fantasy, framed in comic book language: 'When I get fit and grow bionic arms, The whole world's gonna wish it hadn't been born'. It is an irreverent but expertly duplicitous lyric, as triumphant as it is ridiculous.

The band, infused with new confidence and direction, were beginning to enjoy playing live again. Typically playful, Paul developed the practice of walking round and round his microphone with his guitar lead. Eventually the stand would be pulled over, forcing Paul's guitar roadie Ivey to rush on stage and untangle it. All so Paul could repeat the process a few moments later. Apparently it did not occur to the bemused soul that Paul might be doing this on purpose.

The band's third major domestic tour was highly potent and successful. Typically it would finish with a thunder flash affect to accompany set-closer 'A Bomb In Waldour Street', and Weller's cry of "Apocalypse!". The band would re-emerge through the smoke for their encores, with 'David Watts' the usual finale.

The Jam's label mates of the time included the recalcitrant Siouxsie & The Banshees, and Sham 69. With the latter they often shared gigs and became friendly with members backstage. The possible exception of noted rentagob Jimmy Pursey aside. Master Pursey encountered the wrath of the usually implacable Rick Buckler at the Polydor A&R department. Pursey was dominating the stereo with his new single, as pleased as punch with its customary artistry and beguiling lyrical insight. However, no-one else in the room was similarly charmed. Rick, trying to conduct a discussion with Jam press representative Geoff Dean, got so annoyed at the actions of Pursey he walked over to the stereo and threw the offending record across the room. Which caused a brief moment of anxiety: 'I suddenly remembered how much bigger Pursey was than me.

However, he merely replaced the record carefully in its sleeve and skulked out of the room. I was dead relieved'.

CHAPTER FIVE

So You Finally Got What You Wanted

The beginning of 1979 saw the Jam's first major European tour. The dates in France and Belgium proved successful, but playing the Star Club in Hamburg turned out to be something of a disaster. Primarily booked in deference to the Beatles appearances there a decade and a half earlier, The Jam's visit turned out to be terribly organised, with little pre-publicity. And then they discovered that it wasn't actually *the* Star Club. The original had been knocked down and they had built a facsimile across the road.

April saw their third tilt at America, and their first Canadian dates. Having learned the lessons of the last nightmare, the band were booked into club dates much more suitable to their stature in the country. However, the net result was still a loss of about five or six thousand pounds, caused primarily by the band shipping their own monitors with them.

America could still be a hard place to figure out. In Chicago, they played alongside Steve Jones' and Paul Cook's Professionals at a venue which was once Al Capone's favourite dance hall. By which time, presumably,

The JAM

the ex-Pistols had forgotten to honour dead Sidney's vow to level Paul's head. Unfortunately for both parties, it was in an area of the city that had long since gone downhill. 'We remember the gig being great, but actually being quite frightened getting to and from it.'

By the time they had reached the Canadian stretch of dates, Bruce remembers telephoning home to Pat and announcing that he'd had enough, and was coming home. 'You'd get like that now and again. Sometimes with touring things would just get on top of you. I don't think I would ever actually have done something like that though, just packed my bags and left'. Not that tour manager Ken Wheeler didn't enjoy a little panic when, after Bruce had announced his intentions, he went in to his room to find him gone.

Bruce was not the only one to get fed up. For all his stated disinterest, American tours continued to cause Paul anxiety. Often feeling bullied into being there at all, rash statements, such as those made first time on stage at CBGB's, were not exactly infrequent.

On the Los Angeles leg of the 'Setting Sons' tour, Bruce and Rick were caught amid a fracas which erupted at the Rainbow Club, a popular local drinking hole. Both were forced to make a rapid exit. Originally finding themselves in the eye of the storm, they somehow managed to burrow clear of the escalating violence. Which was just as well, by the time they had got outside, approaching sirens indicated the arrival of the notorious LAPD. Not wishing to explain away the evening's activities, they happened upon two accommodating ladies who allowed them to jump in to their car shortly before the law arrived. 'I don't know if they knew who we were', muses Rick, 'but we were grateful for their presence.'

The Jam's touring culture was dominated by alcohol.

The JAM

Dickie Bell, who had proved an effective match for the band on drinking adventures, joined them in one European bar for a session on cocktails. The revellers were more impressed by the visual splendour of the red, green and blue concoctions than any merit of taste. Consequently, Dickie became very ill. Bruce and Rick had to help accompany him up the stairs to his room. 'This being the very guy meant to be looking after us', shrugs Rick.

Thinking they had made a reasonable job of getting Dickie bedded down for the night, the band retired to their own rooms; Rick's being next door to the errant tour manager. However, only ten minutes had elapsed before an ear-piercing scream dragged Rick from his bed and in to the adjacent suite. Dickie Bell stood stock still in the room, his trousers undaintily flagging around his ankles. All eyes turned towards the roof.

It later transpired that Dickie had decided to go toilet before retiring. Unfortunately, his sight impaired, he had chosen the bidet as receptacle. And this particular bidet happened to have a very strong jet on it. So as soon as Dickie attempted to pull what he thought to be the flush, the jet had simply hoisted his turd straight into the air and lashed it to the ceiling.

As Rick, then Bruce entered, the unappetising projectile was slowly becoming detached. All that they could do for the bemused Dickie was to advise him to move out of the way until gravity had worked its miracle.

It was also down to the responsible Dickie Bell's drinking prowess that Rick Buckler missed a flight to Belgium. The band had just played Hammersmith Odeon and the tour manager came over to Rick's house in Lightwater for a drink or five. Which was a mistake, because Rick had umpteen bottles of red plonk stocked up which he had saved from the tour's rider. Dickie, a former wine-waiter, had persuaded him of the merits of the grape on tour. Rick tended to hang around Dickie because his palate was superb, and whichever town they found themselves in, he was sure to know of the best local eatery. However Dickie, for all his sophistication, was not above adopting the gung-ho approach to drinking when the opportunity beckoned. He had already shaved all his hair off on tour after losing one drinking wager. Consequently the two of them stayed up all night until they had drank their way through all but one of the eighteen bottles.

When they woke the next morning, they proceeded to polish off that remaining bottle in the taxi. However, when they reached the airport, they were too late for the flight. Inconsolable at the thought of their late arrival, they decided: 'Well, we might as well wait in the bar'. By the time they had managed to arrange a standby flight, arrived in Belgium and picked up the courtesy car to take them to the gig, the Kinks were already playing at the Festival. John Weller was alerted to the fact that they had arrived, and that his drummer and tour manager were having a mud-fight in the middle of the arena. He presumably also thanked his lucky stars that The Jam weren't scheduled to appear until the following day.

It was such gluttony that forced Rick on the wagon for a short time. Unlike Bruce and Paul, Rick never drank during the day when on tour. 'I just couldn't handle all-day drink-ing, I would just fall straight asleep all the time'. However, he did his best to catch up in the evening. His preferred red wine, he was eventually advised, was also contributing to the health problems he had been having.

Dickie Bell was a positive angel, however, compared to the crew boss who shall remain nameless. A Scottish gent - whom we shall call Jock, as everybody else did - was in charge of the cast and crew for an early 1980 jaunt in America. Being as well disposed to alcohol and cheap sexual thrills as the rest of the touring party, he teamed up with a hooker on the East Coast leg of the tour. Unfortunately for him, and the rest of the entourage, he made the archetypal "crew boss drunk with lady of the night" error. He fell blithely asleep after indulging his passion. When he woke up over £1,000, basically the entire crew's wages, had disappeared. Jock would have been the laughing stock of the tour had the crew, to a man, not wished to castrate him.

Rick, who over the years had become the most accident prone member of the trio, nearly never returned from the States after that tour. Pissed and partying round an outdoor swimming pool in Phoenix, some bright spark decided it might be fun to get the drummer wet. Roadie Alan grabbed hold of him and together they tumbled into the pool.

Unfortunately for Rick nobody knew that he couldn't swim, or those that did had become too drunk to remember. Eventually, after bobbing up and down and flailing like a paddle steamer, it finally occurred to his boisterous audience that he might be experiencing difficulties. Alan redeemed his earlier actions by fishing him out. Not before Rick had swallowed about half of the pool however. Chastened by the experience, and with a few days spare on the itinerary, Rick decided to spend the rest of his time in Phoenix in the shallow end, learning the breaststroke .

Back in England, relentless touring continued with the 'Jam Em In' tour. Operating from the 4th of May to June 6th, the first night saw the band contending with an interview from Gary Bushell, known affectionately to the band as "double chin and tonic". Then Sounds writer Bushell would go on to become the Sun's TV columnist, and was derided by Bruce Foxton thus: 'We knew you went to the gig, cos we

The JAM

saw your chin hanging over the balcony like a net curtain'. He was similarly lambasted for arriving in a courtesy limousine from Polydor's PR department. The Jam were still keen to avoid the ostentatious trappings of their rapidly increasing fame.

They remained, however, ever keen to return the compliment to their ferocious fan base. At the Westfield Cricketers Pub in 1979, they performed a small 'thankyou' affair for friends and their local following. It is remembered with clarity as the last time they worked with their regular PA crew, for after the gig they purchased the unit. One of the guys who co-owned it was the son of a director of Marks & Spencers. Following his death he inherited a small fortune and was flying off to the States to spend it.

The Cricketer locals, meanwhile, didn't take too kindly to their territory being overrun by a bunch of mods and Jam fans. One of the locals was becoming rather over-heated, and Kenny Wheeler had to be delegated to take him outside and give him a slap in the car-park. It turned out to be an ill-starred night. Bruce picks up the story:

'While we were on stage, Nikki Weller (Paul's sister, who would later run The Jam's fan club operation) somehow got involved in an argument with another girl concerning Paul. Pat (Bruce's girlfriend and later wife) was standing next to Nikki, and was picked upon with the result that she had some of her hair pulled out. I only found out about this after the show. On learning of this I was quite annoyed and became intent on finding the guilty parties and pulling their heads off. After some frantic moments searching, I decided I had identified the girl and her boyfriend. Of course I would never hit a woman, but the boyfriend, I thought, was fair revenge.

However, it resulted in the person I picked upon not only

getting the better of me, and ripping all my shirt buttons off, but also he was totally unconnected with the fracas. All I remember after that was being pulled over the bar by security and making a quick exit.'

Unbeknown to Bruce, during the exchanges inside the building, a friend of his had seen the incident and done his best to 'protect Pat's honour'. He was unceremoniously thrown out of the club as reward for his pains. Bruce discovered him dusting himself off outside as he went to step in to an urgently ordered cab. Not realising what had happened, Bruce could only shout 'Where the fuck were you' at his pal. Which just about rounded off a frankly bizarre series of misunderstandings.

Bruce had meanwhile hooked up with the Vapors. A small distance down the road from Woking was a town called Godalming. A pub there nicknamed Scratchers by regulars, hosted bands every Sunday evening. Bruce often ventured down as it was something to do on a quiet night. He saw the Vapors playing one night, and began chatting with fellow bass player Steve Smith. Eventually they came up with the idea of Bruce managing them. However, The Jam were then very busy, and Bruce decided it would be too much to take on his own. He consequently asked John Weller if he would be interested in joint responsibility for the group. It worked out that John would manage the business side of their affairs, while Bruce would try to look after the artistic side. 'That boiled down to personnel skills and trying to avoid the tantrums rock bands find themselves susceptible to. Which, ahem, I know all about'.

The Vapors were indeed a capable and exciting prospect. They are still fondly remembered in the UK for their major hit 'Turning Japanese', an ode to the Far East and masturbation, still revisited by Radio and TV whenever an item on the Orient turns up. However, the rest of their material is

103

just as strong, and it is a great shame that the pressure got
to singer Dave Fenton in the way it did. 'He began to blame
the rest of his band when the pressure to follow up the hit
mounted and it all got a bit messy. Which was a shame, cos
they definitely had the songs'. The rest of Bruce's days with
the Vapors are remembered as 'uncomfortable'.

In their time, however, the Vapors profited greatly from the
patronage of Bruce and The Jam. They became regular
touring companions: which lay them open to the usual
barrage of pranks and abuses. While on stage Paul, Rick
and Bruce took great pleasure in taping their personal
effects to the roof of their dressing room. But the main butt
of jokes was Vapors tour manager, Tony Newman. He was
once dispatched with instructions to purchase copies of
each week's Melody Maker, Sounds and New Musical
Express. The unfortunate soul came in for some gleeful
ribbing when he returned with sixteen copies, one for each
member of the party. 'Plonker!', cite Rick and Bruce in
unison. The headline band decided Mr Newman, who is
remembered as looking like a natural victim in the Woody
Allen mode, had 'spent far too long trying to ingratiate
himself with us'. He was promptly gaffer taped to a chair
outside the Swan Hotel in Newcastle. Once again, alcohol is
involved in the tale somewhere.

The Jam, back on their own terms, continued to plough
what would become one of the most evocative furrows of
pop music singledom with 'Strange Town' and 'When
You're Young'. The latter was a powerful and sympathetic
portrait of youth, Weller's 'My Generation': It also seemed
to be a well-directed kick against those musicians in the
punk movement who were a long way away from the
teenage years they were singing about. It also drew paral-
lels to the punk explosion and its musical empowerment
'You're fearless and brave, you can't be stopped when
you're young, You used to fall in love with everyone, Any

guitar and any bass drum'.

However, it soon gives way to the stinging, unavoidable 'But you find out life isn't like that'. Vic Coppersmith Heaven remembers that Weller was very intense in the studio, and junked a lot of material early. At one point his impatience nearly led him to drop 'Tube Station' when it wasn't working. 'Going Underground' was cut on 40 acetates before the final version, while mixing for both 'Tube' and 'Strange Town' was an equally laborious process. The length of time spent on each was indicative of Heaven's quality threshold, the results of which ultimately served The Jam well.

Polydor weren't always as supportive or trusting. After two versions of 'When You're Young' proved unsatisfactory, Paul, John and Vic were dragged in for a showdown with the managing director of Polydor. He said Smith would have to go in favour of a name American producer. Paul Weller put his foot down hard and that was the end of that.

Despite his defence of Vic, Paul was beginning to have problems with his producer's meticulous approach. Heaven was an absolute perfectionist, a totally implacable foil. 'Vic would be quite prepared to spend time getting the sound absolutely right, even if it was something insignificant like the difference of the drum sound in different rooms'. And if the studio costs were escalating through the roof, that was none of Vic's concern.

'Strange Town' had moved the band further away from traditional Mod and Punk values, with a quasi-psychedelic feel and vocal effect borrowed liberally from the Buzzcocks' 'What Do I Get'. The video for the single was one of the band's favourites, simply because it was shot as a straight, simulated performance. 'Which', concludes Bruce, 'was actually what we were good at. We hated all this pretending to be actors lark. We were never really a video band. We always preferred the live stuff'. Similarly 'When You're Young' was shot in the Queens Park bandstand next to Kingswood Avenue. Once again intended to replicate the feel of The Jam live, like most of the band's videos it was cut on a very tight budget. 'We could never understand the point of spending thousands on a video when it might never be shown. So if we had to do them, they were done as cheaply as possible. It was only later on in the eighties when you "had to have an expensive video" to get anywhere'.

The enthralling b-side to 'Strange Town' was 'Butterfly Collector', Weller's voice magnificent in its bittersweet detachment. The song, in actual fact, concerns Paul's liaison with 'super groupie' Sue Catwoman. Paul had originally come back to the band with lewd stories about talcum power and baby oil, before he eventually tired of the woman for the reasons outlined in the song.

However, it wasn't either the band's nor Paul's only example of 'playing away from home'. Rick remembers one early London gig, after Paul had started seeing Gill, when he had to be pulled from the toilet where he was engaged in a sexual act with a fan. The Jam were due on stage and Paul, smiling like the proverbial Cheshire Cat, had barely managed to do his flies up.

A little less fraught and better organised than the Cricketer's 'thank you' event, were the 'John's Boys' secret gigs in November 1979. Taking place at the Marquee and Nashville a couple of weeks before the main tour happened, they would be well attended by both hard-core fans and journalists 'in the know'. It allowed the latter their first preview of The Jam's new album played live. Sessions had started in August at Townhouse studios, with the eventual release tied down to October 1979.

CHAPTER SIX

Sup Up Your Beer And Collect Your Fags

I f 'All Mod Cons' had earmarked The Jam as one of Britain's most important groups, 'Setting Sons' demonstrated further progression in the possibilities of their sound. Weller would quite quickly disown the album's contents however, because of its lyrical detachment. Pure reportage was a songwriting medium he may have been ready to shed, certainly, but some of the band's strongest songs are housed in its grooves.

At the time Weller was reading a lot of 'classic' working class literature like Alan Sillitoe and George Orwell. After a short story by Dave Waller, he had hatched the plan of using 'Setting Sons' as a concept piece. The central theme concerned three characters, one to each side of the political spectrum of Weller, based loosely on real people. One character is a revolutionary, the other a businessman. Only five of the LPs songs turned out to concern these characters however. When the press reported The Jam's plans for a concept album there were too many scared letters from fans not wishing the band to be confused with ELP.

'Setting Sons' was the band's first album not to be completed under time constraints. The pressure this time was on actually writing songs in the studio for the first time. 'We would stay up until the early hours of the morning, working out what we would record the next day. Then we'd get up, record, and spend the following evening repeating the process, planning the day after. Most of the songs were sort of written but the arrangements and parts were worked out in-between. Basically, everything we recorded was used somewhere, we never rejected songs, apart from the aborted third album, after we'd decided to record them'.

Budgeted for £60,000, the recording costs for 'Setting Sons' eventually weighed in at double that amount. Writing in the studio was a new discipline, and one which brought with it much greater costs. The block booking for the sessions saw that money was wasted every time the band knocked off in the evening. Which was generally when Paul decided he wanted to go home and get his tea before Coronation Street started. There were other extravagances however: 'Everybody was eating there during the day, and even the roadies were getting taxis home at the end of the evening'.

In addition, Paul was becoming progressively more frustrated at Vic Coppersmith Heaven's recording technique. Whereas before his reassuring, unflappable methods had helped balance the group, Paul was now beginning to feel that he was actually holding things up. The fact that the budget swelled so steeply added to his discontent.

'Private Hell' was a good example of Weller writing under pressure. Partially inspired by Joy Division of all people, it is an endearing attempt to look in to the world of women - previously barren ground for the lyricist. 'Saturday's Kids' returned to boyish pride but was a somewhat misinterpreted, Pursey-esque rant. It includes the giveaway line

The JAM

'Hate the system, What system?'. By now we were safe to assume the proximity of Weller's tongue and cheek. There is certainly less of the seamless feel of 'All Mod Cons', with some of the songs letting the side down. The inclusion of the cover of 'Heatwave', for instance, was primarily through lack of original material. Not, as many concluded, for light relief. The band were also devastated to discover that the track had been chosen over much better cuts as the album's promotional single in the US.

However, the centre piece of the album was the storming 'Eton Rifles'. The 'Sup up your beer, and collect your fags' line parodies the 'revolution begins at closing time' brigade, exemplified by the Citizen Smith member of the concept trio. It was also an accurate reflection of Weller's own concerns, that long-term political objectives should be subjugated to the short term need for the working class to have fun. Honest and playful, it was the second of Weller's truly great songs.

One of the most interesting tracks to record was 'Little Boy Soldiers'. Bruce was let loose on the cello: 'I'd never played a cello before, and even though the chords were simple, I had to mark them down on the fretboard with chalk. And I was paranoid that somebody would rub them off and I wouldn't be able to play along'. Rick, meanwhile, was having his own troubles on the same track: 'We decided the sound of broken bottles should be used at the end of 'Little Boy Soldiers', so I raided the studio kitchen of about a dozen used wine bottles. We tied them up in a carrier bag, so that it would save having to sweep up broken glass around the studio afterwards. So I swung the bag against the wall and the whole package exploded, all these shards of glass flying everywhere. After all that, I'd managed to cock it up and do it out of time anyway'. As well as sweeping up, the sound engineers thus had the problem of 'dropping in' the recording of the broken glass in to its correct

The JAM

spot.

'By the time 'Settings Sons' came around, we'd got quite a regulated routine. We had set times to make a start, and times for meals and stuff like that. Our system was to try and get the backing tracks - drums, bass, and guitar down first. Quite often that would work first take. But we never did the backing tracks all at the same time, we'd take two or three and then worry about the overdubs and vocals. But generally it was always easier if the songs had been played out on the road beforehand'.

The distinctive front cover art work for 'Setting Sons' was taken from a sculpture by Benjamin Clemens, 'The St. John's Ambulance Bearers'. It stands in the Imperial War Museum in London next to the less dramatic Cenotaph which was originally to have been used. Both of which accurately reflect the sombre tones of the record the final sleeve enveloped.

Behind the scenes, Weller was still behaving like the class-conscious upstart whose character had been so apparent in Woking. Rick had decided it would be a good idea to purchase his first house. To Paul this was a horrific gesture, and Rick endured constant ribbing as to his 'establishment' status. This despite the fact that the rather plush flat Paul was now sharing with Gill actually cost a great deal more in rent than Rick's mortgage.

Other contradictions in Paul's character were evident in domestic life. 'At one point he decided that he would have his flat carpeted in plain black, presumably to signify post-war austerity, 'pop art' or some other such philosophy'. Everybody else, of course, was using flowered designs or shagpile at this point, so in pursuit of the sombre and mini-malist, Paul once again ended up shelling out much more than was the going rate.

110

The JAM

One of the ripest lines in 'Eton Rifles' runs: 'We were no match for their untamed wit, though some of the lads said they'll be back next week'. This half-apologetic assertion mirrors Weller's own class consciousness, black carpets notwithstanding, to a tee. The song nearly became self-fulfilling prophecy when 'The Right To Work' march was jeered at by Eton schoolboys.

During the recording sessions Rick spent one anxious evening trying to avoid the attentions of a particularly ardent bunch of Mod fans. Forty of them flocked over to the studios and refused to believe that The Jam were not on site. Having pushed past a placatory Coppersmith Heaven, they satisfied themselves that the band were probably in the toilets and invited them over to the pub for a beer when they had finished.

More serious for Rick were the injuries sustained when old mucker Chris Parry arranged to borrow his drum kit for another band he was managing. Afterwards Rick and the tour manager left Malden Studios to go for a drink at Crispin's Wine Bar in Ealing. They came back to the studio, predictably, 'silly drunk'. Deciding he had become irritated by something or other, Rick kicked through a plate glass window in the complex. The injuries were not as severe as they might have been; merely splinters of glass in the ankle. However, John Weller was not amused at his percussionist's errant behaviour. The band were about to play a prestigious gig at the Rainbow to boot, and Rick was firmly informed 'to stand still with his hands in his pockets for the foreseeable future'.

Which is why, incidentally, pictures of Rick taken at this juncture will reveal to the observant the fact that one of his feet, bandaged beneath his shoe, appears bigger than the other.

The JAM

Rick was also the band member, seemingly, most likely to miss his flight. It nearly happened coming home from Los Angeles on one occasion, particularly galling for Rick as, 'After a six-week tour, what everybody was desperate to do was come home. However, the inevitable party the night before at the end of a tour would often cause problems'. Waking up bleary eyed, Rick discovered he had been left at the hotel with a ticket and all his equipment and possessions had been loaded on the plane. Which made the mad-dog rush to get to the plane on time worthwhile.

If Rick ever experienced difficulty with the tour itinerary, on stage things ran smoothly thanks to drum roadie Wally. Although Wally is remembered as being an excellent crew member, he did have his quirks. While the band were on stage, he would take his place behind Bruce's amps, and unfold his little deck chair. 'Then', continues Bruce, 'on would go his favourite, moth-eaten tartan slippers, and out would come the paper. And he would spend the whole gig sat there'. His implacable poise certainly helped to bring the lads down after a performance. After sweating their way through the excitement of a Jam gig for over an hour, with the fans going completely nuts, the trip backstage would inevitably see them nodding hello to Wally, whose eyes would barely move from his newspaper.

Paul's roadie Ivey, was a little more easy to wind up, as we have already seen. However, on one occasion he came perilously close to losing more than his dignity. Sitting behind Paul's stack of AC30's where he'd been fixing a slight problem, he lifted his head up just as Paul crashed his guitar down on the amp. Swinging his face out of the way just in time, it came close enough to decapitation to make him a little wary of Paul's stage behaviour in the future.

MORE PROMO

ME

AND ME

PAUL IN A PENSIVE MOOD

DOING A EUROPEAN TV SHOW

LIVE AGAIN

THOSE JACKETS AGAIN!

TOP OF THE POPS

PAUL DURING THE SHOOTING OF THE
'ABSOLUTE BEGINNERS' VIDEO

AND THEY SAID NO-ONE WOULD EVER KNOW

VIC COPPERSMITH HEAVEN AT THE CONTROLS

TOP OF THE POPS AGAIN

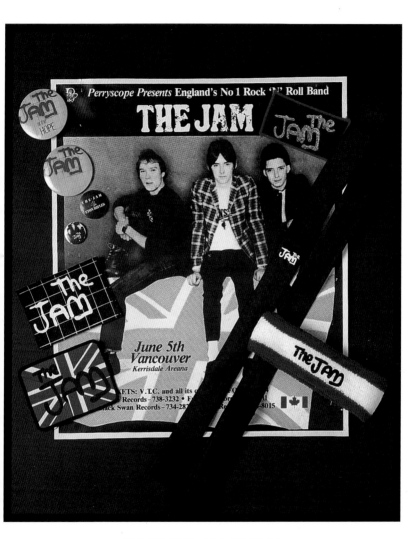

REMEMBER ALL OF THIS

RARE MOMENTS OF RELAXATION

A FRIENDLY GAME OF CARDS

ON THE TOUR BUS WITH STEVE NICOLL & STEVE THOMAS

CHAPTER SEVEN

What You See Is What You Get

The band's reservations about 'Setting Sons' arose primarily out of the fact that they had been unable to properly break in the songs on stage. 1980, however, saw The Jam unable to put a foot wrong, commercially or artistically. A new album was preceded in the Spring by 'Going Underground'.

The single was originally intended as a double a-side, with the magnificent 'Dreams Of Children' getting lost in the rush somewhere. 'Underground' was the closest Weller came to punk's nihilism in any of his material, an absolute rejection of his surroundings. In truth it was not as good a song as any of the previous three singles, each of which had revealed quite separate progressions. 'Going Underground' was much more traditional Jam fare.

Following its release the Jam found themselves on their fourth US tour. They had arrived on American soil on the 22nd of February, and completed the East Coast leg before travelling across to San Francisco and Los Angeles. John Weller had been informed via the telephone of the advance orders ensuring 'Going Underground' would strike a healthy chart position.

The JAM

They just happened to be in Los Angeles again, staying at the Sunset Marquee in Hollywood, when the news broke. Legendary in rock 'n' roll circles as the hotel to hang out at, wild parties were seemingly obligatory. Built, almost classically, to encompass a swimming pool at its centre (handy for the disposal of TV's), the band arrived having heard their fill of drug, sex and drink stories whose origins could be traced to a band's residency at this fabled site. When John Weller predicted their highest chart return in the UK, it was time to party, and the venue seemed ideal.

John Weller was on the phone confirming the news. His charges in the background were hooting for him to hang up and join them on the piss. John, being as resolute as ever, could not be extracted from his conversation. So the boys sneaked down the corridor, 'found a suitable length of wire, and cut it. We all felt emotional and just wanted to get drunk and celebrate a bit' Their quiet act of vandalism was but a simple ruse in order to be able to charge up to John and insist that now he had been cut off, he didn't have any excuse not to join them at the bar.

However, when they returned to reception after a brief tour of the area's watering holes, they were astonished to find that The Jam were banned from staying at the hotel. There was much head shaking in the vacinity. Not only had the band been told that throwing a full suite in the swimming pool was de rigeur, they had also seen with their own eyes how practically every item of furniture in the building had been stuck back together following breakage. It was a DIY enthusiasts dream. Visitors practically had to screw their bed together before they would dare sleep on it.

The band were secretly quite pleased with the achievement of an actual ban from the Sunset Marquee. They were only a little aggrieved that it hadn't been for something a little more substantial than snipping a telephone wire.

The JAM

However, nobody had grasped quite how well the single had done. The Jam were actually en route from Houston to Austin when 'Going Underground' debuted at number 1. It was the first time such a thing had happened since Slade performed the feat with 'Cum On Feel The Noize'. The free EP with initial copies combined with huge advance orders to ensure its success.

Some in the industry pointed out that its release date allowed more sales to be taken into account during its first week on sale. This was interpreted as a clever marketing device on Polydor's behalf, and one which contributed significantly to the fact that it cornered the top spot. This was plainly untrue, it had sold enough to gain it pole position on advance orders alone, before the supporting titles, never mind the free EP, had even been announced.

The band opted for a dash of pop star posing to celebrate the success of 'Going Underground'. They managed to escape the rigours of the rest of the tour by finding a loophole: 'After all, it was the American South and we weren't exactly big business over there, because it was the first time we'd really been in the region and in America each state is like cracking a different country'. Instead they flew from Austin to Washington, then over to the East Coast for a plane back to Blighty. The idea being to 'enjoy some of the adulation while it lasted'.

Their celebrations took the form two Easter gigs at the Rainbow over the bank holiday. These sets have achieved almost mythical status in the memories of The Jam fans who attended. Triumphant at being back in England, not to mention their conquering of the charts, no less than five encores were unveiled on the opening night. The audience celebrated their return by ritually wrecking the seating, almost in deference to the band's origins.

The Jam

The bulk of 1980 was taken up with pushing The Jam's name and music into new territories. May's shows in Spain and the Pink Pop Festival in Holland, then their first five dates in Japan, sandwiched an appearance at the Loch Lomond Festival and three other home dates.

The Loch Lomond Festival had become an annual event in Scotland's rock diary. The Jam's appearance was triumphant, though Rick learned from the promoter that nothing was likely to match the previous year's antics. One fan had turned up and indulged himself in various chemical substances. 'Off his box', he managed to wander off course until he found himself a bolt hole to sleep in.

The following morning he awoke to a flurry of lights and noise. He reportedly shouted something about teddy bears in his ongoing delirium. In actual fact he had spent the night sleeping in the enclosure of a nearby bear park. And the cuddly grizzlies who had just discovered his presence were about to wander over and see if he would pass for breakfast. Luckily for the besieged music fan, the warden had spotted what was happening and managed to fire off a tranquillising dart at the advancing bear.

Equally as bizarre, however, was the Turku Festival in Finland, which took place on the 9th of August. Set by a river, the local Norwegian contingent had decided to set up their own stage, basically amounting to the back of a lorry, in competition with the main platform. The Jam played, alongside Dave Edmunds, while over the other side, the Norwegians began to fight amongst themselves over who should be the final, headlining band.

The fights spilled over on to the main stage as the violence spread. Thankfully for The Jam, the band had played their set and taken their equipment and were about to leave. Shortly afterwards, the rampaging crowd had physically dismantled the main stage, and in a fit of pique, thrown all the equipment in to the river. Apparently in Finland memories still survive of panicking roadies clutching manfully on to PA bins as they floated away down the river.

Not that all of Scandinavia proved so hostile. During their November tour of Sweden and Norway, which preceded dates in Holland, Belgium and Germany, they played at a remarkable event at an indoor fairground at the Christiana Centre. They were allowed into the building an hour or so early to sound check, but spent most of their time checking out the rides.

'Start', a plea for communication and understanding, would follow 'Going Underground' in to pole position a few months later. Built around a riff which shared strong similarities with the Beatles' 'Taxman', there were those who accused Weller of opportunism. 'Apart from the first notes, the rest of the bass line is quite different. The idea that its a rip-off is a bit of a misconception as far as I'm concerned' notes Rick. While the press felt they could nail the band for plagiarism, the band never tried to hide the fact that the song was heavily influenced by the Fab Four. It was, after all, a track done on the spot with some spare studio time, and actually originated from a riff Bruce was playing around with.

In any case the b-side 'Liza Radley' was more derivative of the Beatles' 'Revolver', it was just harder to tie it to anything specific. 'At the time Paul and I were just listening to that album all the time on tour, so it probably just rubbed off'. Polydor, in their finite wisdom had wanted 'Pretty Green' to be the single, going so far as to press up sleeves. The Jam won the day, and their opinion was born out by the success of the record.

From the Easter Rainbow dates onwards, the band had

added the services of Merton Parka Mick Talbot for their live shows. He would later form the Style Council with Paul. He bolstered The Jam's sound with keyboards for the first time since the abortive employment of Bob Gray. A move which predicted the wider musical sweep that 'Sound Affects' would boast.

The band entered Townhouse Studios in Shepherds Bush in July 1980, working for three months in total on the band's fifth album. They might have appreciated a break after the rigour of their huge recording and touring commitments, but Polydor were having none of it. The autumn tour needed to pin itself on the back of a new album, and so the band were told to go away and write and record one.

Despite the time pressures, the sessions for the album would actually finish one day early. 'The studio was all booked and paid for', recalls Rick, 'and we'd already finished. So we spent the whole day pratting around recording insects and flies. Just generally wasting the day'. The fly is actually recorded for posterity just before 'Music For The Last Couple'.

'Vic was so easy going it wasn't true. We were all quite frantic and he was just the opposite. Between the three of us, we ran out of patience with him some times. Paul would quite often just go: "Right, I'm not doing it again". Vic's approach was a bit slow and Paul wanted it down there and then. And if it didn't happen he would storm off or just stand there and insist he wasn't going to do his vocal or whatever. But Vic did help balance the group'.

Bruce's memories of Vic are compounded by those of Rick, who notes that Vic 'Used to wind up John Weller something rotten. We had to have the phone taken out of the studio at one point, cos if Vic got on it he would be there for hours. God alone knows who he was phoning. We'd be hanging around waiting, and John would come in and shout "Let's fucking well get things moving, we're paying for all this studio time". But that was all water off a duck's back to Vic. "Yeh, sure John, I'll just finish this call and I'll be with you in a minute"'.

The three verses on the back of 'Sound Affects' are taken from Shelley's 'Mask Of Anarchy'. It demonstrated Weller's wider reading, with several of the songs related to specific literary sources. 'Man In The Corner Shop', an agnostic religious ode, drew on some of the bogus ancient wisdom expressed as 'spiritual' in books like Geoffrey Ashe's 'Camelot And The Vision Of Albion' and 'King Arthur's Albion'. For Rick Buckler, however, there were much more practical considerations: 'We recorded that on a Monday morning and I had the most godawful hangover. I remember sitting there dreading having to hit the drums, cos every time I did the noise made me feel physically sick. By about mid-day I was like jelly, but after that they were doing the guitar overdubs and I'd got throught it. I was very relieved, because at last I could go and find some-where to sleep'.

The optimism of 'Sound Affects', easily discernible from its pithy forerunner, was partially influenced by further reading of Orwell. In particular, 'Homage To Catalonia'. The passages describing the workers' egalitarian society established during the Spanish Civil War promised light at the end of the tunnel for Weller.

In interviews he also asserted that 'Sound Affects' was the end to his 'sitting on the fence' period. A case of reacting directly to music press criticism, it nevertheless invoked a new depth to Weller's lyricism. Previously the songs had swelled from a strong narrative base, but now the writing was becoming increasingly expressionistic (the preserve of the middle classes). 'That's Entertainment', cited by many as Weller's greatest moment, was a wonderful journey through working class, decaying England. Visions of despair and the empty gestures of a rotten soul roll by with the soothing hook line only sharpening the dull ache of it all. Like 'Tube Station', it had been written in a matter of minutes.

To the band's dismay, it was released as a single in Europe by Polydor and imported in such quantities that it made the charts. Such was the popularity of the band in the early 80s.

Dabbling in funk, 'Pretty Green' was partially inspired by Michael Jackson, and 'Start' was present in remixed form. 'Music For The Last Couple' is one of only two group compositions on the record, Bruce taking a reluctant back-seat on the songwriting front.

'Sound Affects' is Paul Weller's favourite Jam album. It wins through not for the consistency which had marked earlier efforts, but for the individual strengths of several songs. 'Set The House Ablaze' recounts the experience of friendships broken as the protagonist joins the army. It is markedly similar in tone to Stiff Little Finger's 'Tin Soldiers', whom Foxton would join. On 'Monday' - 'I will never be embarrassed about love again' was a terse, post-punk declaration, and another great song.

If 'Sound Affects' was The Jam's 'Revolver', the masses chorused their approval in shrill tones which almost echoed the heights of Beatlemania. The 'NME' Readers Poll of 1980 saw them bag the lot: 'Best Group', 'Male Singer', 'Guitarist', 'Bass', 'Drums', 'Songwriter', 'Single' ('Going Underground'), Album ('Sound Affects') and Cover Art ('Sound Affects'). This was the third year in a row they'd won the best album award, the second year in which they'd been voted best group. But 1980's show of strength 'by the

Boy's Brigade' was positively domineering.

The band closed 1980 with a typically barnstorming tour of the UK at the top of their form. Their popularity had been built on live potency and the level of intensity hadn't dropped in four years. Plus, they now had the material to do the job properly.

Paul's attitude to The Jam's success, however, continued to be tempered by cynicism and detachment. The band were invited at the tail end of 1980 to the 'Daily Mirror Rock And Pop Awards' ceremony, hosted by Dave Lee Travis. They trooped along expecting to be handed some trinket. 'Well, we were hardly likely to be invited if we weren't going to win anything' ran the logic. So the band huddled together with their girlfriends, until the result of the 'Best Single' nomination was read out by 'star guest' Suzi Quatro.

Unsurprisingly, and deservedly, The Jam took the honours for 'Going Underground'. The house-lights picked out Paul and his cohorts in the audience, preparing for them to come down the aisle and receive their 'prestigious' award. Paul didn't move a muscle. After a couple of embarrassing seconds, Bruce and Rick realised that he had absolutely no intention of budging. 'If Paul had wanted to make some kind of statement then fine, but it might have been nice to inform the rest of us beforehand'.

Rather than cause themselves to look an even bigger spectacle, Bruce and Rick shuffled out of their seats and made their way down the front. Once there they muttered their gratitude to the hapless Dave Lee Travis, who stuck to his script of "Congratulations, its a very, very special award and I hope you carry on winning more and more", before slipping in a small dig about there only being two thirds of the band on stage. 'As if we hadn't noticed' sniffs Bruce. He and Rick mooched straight back to their seats feeling

The Jam

'utterly humiliated'. Throughout the whole fiasco, the ceremony was conducted to a backdrop of 'Going Underground', performed by a massed brass band. 'Now *that* really was weird' reminisces Rick.

Ceremonies and star spangled celeb do's are not all they are cracked up to be, apparently. About the same time Bruce inspected one of his gold discs presented for sales of 'Setting Sons'. The label listing didn't add up to the number of tracks on the record proper. Obviously those responsible had simply stuck the label on top of someone else's record. 'That broke a few illusions' declares Bruce.

Undoubtedly The Jam's stature had risen from that of tertiary punk/mod outfit to fully fledged pop stars. All three members were being pursued for their most intimate details by 'Smash Hits' and the like. Flushed with success, John Weller told Rick quite firmly, that now the band were having number one singles regularly, he really ought to desist from keeping that eleven year old Volvo on the road. It wasn't the style or make that caused concern, more the fact that it so regularly broke down when Rick was meant to be somewhere. Primarily the rehearsal or recording studio. Or even worse, a photo session. While others might have been swanning around in limousines, Rick would still enter stage right, his hands covered in grease, declaring that the steering wheel or some other non-essential gadget had just fallen off his motor. Perhaps purchasing said vehicle off a taxi driver had been Rick's downfall.

For the first time the band's joint account was raided and everybody bought their first new car. And, presumably, Rick and Bruce's parents finally relented on giving their children grief about the precarious nature of their careers.

In actual fact, they had long since done so. Rick remembers his dad being pointed out at a gig as 'the guy with the tour

The Jam

jacket who's 60'. Later Rick discovered a supply of cotton wool in the pockets. His poor father had obviously found his son's delicate musical abilities too loud to bear. Even Bruce's grandmother, pushing the eighty mark, attended one of the London shows.

The band were invited to support another good cause on February 16, 1981. Woking YMCA was short on funds and who better to bolster the coffers than the town's favourite sons. The very eminent Ms Mary Phillips presented The Jam with honoury, one year memberships for their trouble. Rick, however, ventured outside the gig only to discover two young fans attempting to rip the number plate off his TR6 as a souvenir.

The odd charity gig aside, the trio were never moral paragons. Touring Europe in support of 'Sound Affects' in March 1981, the band were enjoying a rare day off in Amsterdam. Partaking of a drink from the mini-bar in Rick's room, they saw their way through its entire contents with ease. Paul volunteered to go and retrieve a few drinks from his room. Which, everyone decided, was an absolutely splendid idea. The next thing that Bruce and Rick heard, however, was a horrible squeaking sound coming down the corridor of the hotel. Paul had not only brought the drinks, but the drinks cabinet itself, from his room. 'Which seemed such a good idea that I immediately followed suit', concurs Bruce.

Drunken revelry could also make a political point of sorts. Staying at the Blackpool Conference Centre in the early 80s, a few days before the Conservative Party Conference, Paul struck on a wonderful idea. Scuttling off to the toilet with a carrier bag, he regrouped with Bruce and Rick having deposited his business within. Carefully avoiding security, the trio made their way in to the hall prepared for the conference. Underneath the sky blue banners they found the speaker's place at the head table. Whereupon they taped the turd and its container underneath.

Whether or not it would be discovered before the opening gambits of the Tory hierarchy is debatable, but the thought was truly a wonderful one. 'Joe Strummer wouldn't have come up with it in a million years' sniffs Rick.

However, such laddish antics were now the exception rather than the rule. Essentially, Paul now came with his missus in tow. Pat and Lesley, respectively Bruce and Rick's better halves, joined the band on tour infrequently. Occasionally when they were visiting Japan or some other far flung corner it provided a nice opportunity to take them along for the sight-seeing. Together with Paul's girlfriend Gill, they would go off shopping together, or possibly be forced to put on a nice act for an interview. However, the sense of humour inherent in a touring rock 'n' roll band was a bit isolating, and they never really felt part of the action. Gill, however, was a much more regular companion. As she and Paul grew closer, so the distance between he and the rest of the band increased.

'The general rule was that if a band member wanted to bring his girlfriend/wife on tour with the band, then fine, but it came out of your own pocket. But because Paul and Gill were so inseparable a 'job' was created for Gill as the band's unpaid secretary'. She would help out on the merchandise stall as circumstances demanded.

'As soon as Paul came off stage he would be with Gill'. The others decided that the pair of them were seeing far too much of each other, day in day out, but there was nothing they could really say. The unfortunate effect of their tempestuous relationship was that its ebbs and flows affected Paul's mood and, indirectly, their playing performance and songwriting. Both Paul and Gill were eminently capable of 'putting it away' in terms of alcohol. Which was fair enough, as the same was true of every other member of The Jam and most of the road crew. But when Gill and Paul got drunk together they would become progressively louder and more antagonistic. In short it did very little for the balance of the group.

On one occasion Rick remembers being woken up in his hotel bedroom in the small hours to the sound of raised voices. Looking across to another wing of the building, he saw the lights turned on and an almighty row going on. Half-asleep and fed up, he rang down to the hotel reception to complain.

It wasn't until the next morning when Rick wandered down to breakfast that he discovered the source of his nocturnal misery. It was Paul and Gill who had been screaming their lungs out at each other. Paul was heartily denouncing the busy-body who had complained about the noise to his father. Rick prudently decided not to inform Paul who the author of this intrusion really was.

CHAPTER EIGHT

The Flames Grow Higher

By this point in their career the band had long since been forced to employ personal bodyguards. Chris Adoja, Joe Awome and Tony Gibney were the trio in charge of security. Ken Wheeler had overall responsibility, but particularly looked after Paul. 'Even when Paul sloped off for a quiet meal with Gill, Ken would have to tab along and play gooseberry'. Chris Adoja hung around with Rick, while Joe Awome was generally to be seen with Bruce. The bodyguards individual responsibilities were never formalised, however. Tony Gibney laboured under the nickname 'Mono'. So called 'because he was deaf in one ear, and only heard half of what you said'.

Joe Awome was a Commonwealth gold medal winning boxer, and a huge man. To honour his birthday, the group went back to the hotel after their show at the Royal Court in Liverpool. His present was a thoughtfully selected blow-up sex doll. Unfortunately, for all his bulk and size, he found his sexual partner for the evening absolutely impossible to inflate. The big man collapsed in tears of laughter and was forced to abandon the conquest. The reluctant lady spent the rest of the tour strapped under the windscreen wiper of the tour bus.

Which wasn't the only sight to be seen therein. Rigger Ray Salter (known universally as Rat), would regularly sit naked, cross-legged, on the back seats, reading the paper. 'To him it just seemed a perfectly natural thing to do' recalls Rick. In actual fact, he was probably safest where he was. John Weller had long since instigated card schools as the preferred manner of passing time on journeys to and from gigs. 'John had been around a while, and he'd seen a bit of life. I think the idea', muses Rick 'was to give the crew their week's wages, and then see how much John could win back off them the same day. There were some really large pots going, but John knew exactly what he was doing. I think it helped subsidise the whole touring lark'.

By the early 80s The Jam represented a small army on tour. Although, as can be seen, their visual disposition might have seen their presence mistaken for that of a football coach. Returning from a show in Portsmouth on one trek, the tour bus occupants decided to stop off at a Little Chef for a bite and a leak. As was traditional with British Service Stations of the period, a "No Coaches" sign barred the entrance. Too many roadside eateries had seen virtual destruction at the hands of travelling football supporters.

Tour manager Kenny Wheeler quietly entered the establishment to enquire whether or not it would be alright to come in as there were only eight people on the coach. The manager flatly refused. Kenny adopted his best negotiating tone and tried to assure him that the group were just 'nice lads' who wanted something to eat. This manager, however, would not be moved.

Kenny gave up and returned to the coach to give its occupants the bad news. Their opinion of Little Chef's policy, tempered as was usual by colossal hangovers and post-gig hunger, was not the best. 'To prove we were indeed nice

143

The Jam

lads, we asked our driver to cruise past the restaurants front windows whilst all the band 'mooned' at the clientele inside'.

When faced with a similar problem later in the tour, further drastic action was called for. A young manageress at a different service station decided that The Jam touring party was, again, not to be allowed entry to her premises. She became so paranoid and agitated, in fact, that she elected to lock and bolt the restaurant's windows and doors. Desperate for the toilet and cheesed off, this time the entire contents of the tour bus spilled out and stood in line to piss against the restaurant wall. 'You could see the steam cloud about two miles away'.

1981 was the band's quietist, most thoughtful year. Paul had exhausted his most productive writing spell, and after the headlong rush of 'Setting Sons' and 'Sound Affects', the band made a point of not recording an album. They satisfied themselves instead with tours of Europe, Japan, and some seaside UK dates (the 'Bucket and Spade' tour, and the London based CND shows).

Neither of the two singles which did emerge in 1981 were quite from the top flight. 'Funeral Pyre' and 'Absolute Beginners' shared lovely vocal inflections and musical twists but seemed unable to hold themselves together. Lyrically they were all form and no substance. The public reaction compared to the fervour which had greeted 'Going Underground' and 'Start' was relatively moderate - both stalled at number 4 in the charts. The highlight of the two was the extraordinary drum patterns of 'Funeral Pyre' and the 'Absolute Beginners' b-side: 'Tales From The Riverbank'. Based on the unreleased (until 'Extras') 'We've Only Started', it quickly became one of Weller's personal favourites. Its poignant melancholy still makes an occasional appearance in his solo sets.

144

The cover to 'Absolute Beginners' features one of Rick Buckler's photographs, taken from a hotel window. As the drinking binges quietened down on tour, Rick had discovered a talent, or at least enthusiasm for, documenting the band's travels on film. He would later have some of his work featured in a Japanese rock magazine. Rick was not, however, as impressed with the video for 'Beginners': 'That was just really stupid' he frowns, 'We had to chase after this truck with a camera in it, going about 25mph. We were absolutely knackered from running and I couldn't see any relevance to the song or anything else'.

The video for 'Funeral Pyre', meanwhile, was filmed in the sand quarry originally envisaged by H.G. Wells when he wrote 'War Of The Worlds'. Wells had actually lived only a few streets away from the band's home turf. Rick winces at the memory of the video: 'That was good fun, but almost another disaster. The fire brigade were worried about us setting the woods on fire because of the huge bonfire we had to light, and we'd got all our mates in to walk around the set holding flaming torches. And I was petrified in case my drum kit went up in smoke. There were all these embers flying through the air and some of them just burned right through my drum skins.

We couldn't start the bonfire again so we had to get it all filmed while it was burning. We had to keep moving the kit backwards and forwards, and then the wind would change round again. I suppose it must have looked a bit comical, what with the director saying "Yeah, that looks great, just hold it there for a minute". And we were all thinking, fine, but its getting a bit hot here, I'm a bit worried about this. Especially for me, because I had to send my kit back to Premiere to get new skins put on it. It was ruined.'

Of the two singles 'Funeral Pyre' provides the most inter-

The

JAM

esting lyrical subject matter. 'Shed your fears and lose your guilt, Tonight we burn responsibility in the fire'. Weller was increasingly disaffected with the showbiz glamour of 1981's pop scene, Adam and his Ant's second coming mirroring the pomposity of the 70s glam period so reviled by him. 'We basically agreed with most of the things he was saying' confirms Bruce. Paul was not above taking his criticisms of shallow pop in to the letters pages of Record Mirror when his views were challenged.

On October the 5th The Jam flew out to Stockholm to record a television appearance there. Scandinavia, like Los Angeles in the States, regularly threw up some notable oddity. This booking turned out to be 'totally the wrong exposure. It was a cabaret with people sat around the stage at tables, eating. It was like going back on the club circuit. Hugely embarrassing.' Worse still was the Euro show where Paul was confronted with a female interviewer having problems with the lingo. Taking advantage of her stumbling English, when asked to introduce the band's new song he proceeded to announce it as 'Chicken In A Basket'.

Spanish TV, meanwhile, could have given lessons to its British counterparts like 'Top Of The Pops': 'We did one show there', recalls Rick, 'and it was brilliant. Real get in, set up, do one take, then get the hell out job. Next band please. Which was a bit refreshing after spending a whole day doing 'Top Of The Pops' in England. In Spain it was much more lo-tech, all these technicians holding up lights from creaking step-ladders and stuff. In fact that show was the one we did with Van Halen, and their bass player was as pissed as a fart on Jack Daniels and kept walking into things'. It could have been worse. The same year Van Halen vocalist Dave Lee Roth would break his nose on the set of an Italian TV special the hard rockers were filming, having to fly home for surgery before rejoining the tour. He collided with a hanging mirror ball during the execution of a flying squirrel leap. 'Well', muses Bruce, who is just as well known for his on stage athleticism, 'I did manage to put my head through the roof of a gig in Cardiff, but I don't suppose that compares'.

Earlier there had been an appearance on the riotous 'Tiswas', a Saturday morning show purportedly aimed at children. Playing alongside Sad Cafe, The Jam also had the pleasure of inviting their respective girlfriends into the 'Cage'. A noble televisual institution whereby inmates would be held captive for the duration of the programme and become fair game for any character who wished to throw revolting substances at their helpless quarry. The Jam themselves were not above indulging in a spot of 'flan-flinging' for the event.

Weller, meanwhile, had found himself a cause. Having previously turned down 'spokesperson' opportunities like the invitation to appear on 'Nationwide' to talk about the Mod riots, he made his only visible public commitment to CND. His passionate advocacy was emblazoned via the music press: 'Nothing will be achieved all the time we remain separated, but together we can win!'. It was a statement better received in the music press than his advocacy of the monarchy.

From December 12th to the 15th, Weller organised four London shows in support of CND. However, the two gigs at the cavernous Michael Sobell Centre in Finsbury Park were ruined by failing sound, and the CND stalls were knocked over by fans leaving the venue. The Jam followed this by contributing 'Little Boy Soldiers' to the anti-nuclear album 'Life In The European Theatre' in January 1982. The Union Jack button badges had been traded for ones carrying the CND design. Paul also admitted that he'd been a vegetarian for several years and had recently given up

The JAM

alcohol.

Or maybe alcohol had given up on him, as might be indicated by one tale of excess in Japan a few months previously. In Kyoto, Paul was drinking his favoured tipple of vodka. As had become usual, the post-gig binge of drinks backstage and at the hotel bar had proved insufficient. In search of refreshment, Paul reminded his colleagues of a bottle of vodka he was sure he had left in his room. However, he had somewhat underestimated his own state of inebriation. He found himself unable to screw the top of the bottle. Not surprising, in retrospect, as he had already removed the offending item several hours earlier. Undeterred, he managed to bite the top of the bottle neck off in order to gain access to its contents.

The fun did not end there. Although resoundingly half-cut, the band members did at least realise the danger of broken glass going in to the bottle. 'So we hit on the grand scheme of pulling down the hotel curtains in order to sieve the liquid in to a bucket underneath'. No thought of retiring, having drunk approximately two gallons of alcohol, would cross their minds until the final dregs had been drained.

Paul had actually been forced to give up drinking on medical grounds previously in Marseilles, France. After contracting gastric 'flu, Paul's stomach had ballooned and the doctor forced him to swear off the bottle for the three days they were stuck at the hotel. The band remember his moods as being 'shifting'. Bearing in mind the importance alcohol played in the day to day existence of a rock band, such abstinence was certainly painful. His more recent conversion to a teetotal existence was on medical rather than moral grounds too. 'It had got to the stage where his heavy drinking continually resulted in him having total blackouts. He would just get drunk and pass out'.

The JAM

Previously Paul had always suffered terribly from nerves before he went on stage. His answer was to drink moderately during the day to calm himself down, even though he was still prone to throwing up in the toilets a few minutes before he pulled on his guitar strap.

Japan would prove to be one of The Jam's most receptive overseas territories. The band were both excited and confused by its convention and lifestyle. Rick, as hardened a smoker as Paul (it is difficult to find too many photos of them without a tab in their hand), was not enamoured of the fire restrictions. Not being allowed to smoke on stage was a shade too disciplinarian for Rick. So, despite official objections, he would merely wander round the stage with a fire extinguisher in one hand and his cigarette in the other. 'At least they couldn't say there was any danger of me starting a fire then'.

The Jam would enjoy enormous popularity in the Orient. They, in turn, were amazed at the finite detail the Japanese would enter in to, covering every eventuality. Unlike England, activities would be scheduled up to an including every minute of every day. For instance, excerpts from the itinerary of their June 1982 tour give some indication of the discipline it entailed:

6/16 (WED)
TOKYO NIHON
SEINENKAN HALL
TEL: (03)401-0101

10:30 AM HOTEL PICK-UP
11:46 AM LEAVE OSAKA ON HIKARI *160

NEW OTANI
ADD: 4-1 KIYOICHO
CHIYODA-KU TOKYO

TEL: (03) 265-1111
TELEX: J 24719
2:56 PM ARRIVE TOKYO
4:00 PM HOTEL PICK-UP
4:30 PMSOUND CHECK
6:30 PMCONCERT

6/17 (THURS)
AICHI KINRO KAIKAN
TEL: (052)733-1141

12:00 PM HOTEL PICK-UP
12:48 PM LEAVE TOKYO ON HIKARI *115

NAGOYA KANKO HOTEL
ADD: 1-19-30 NISHIKICHO
NAKA-KU NAGOYA
TEL: (052) 231-7711

2:49 PMARRIVE NAGOYA
4:00 PMHOTEL PICK-UP
4:30 PMSOUND CHECK
6:30 PMCONCERT

6/18 (FRI)
DEPARTURE

Though Paul disliked the indiscriminate idolatry aimed at any touring Western band, Japan came closest to replicating the heights of Beatlemania when The Jam were in town. Even the fan letters were of a different class, as this missive from Yuki confirms:

My dearest Rick,
        Hello. I'm a Japanese girl aged 17. I swear that nobody in our country loves The Jam more than I do. And

I'm the luckiest one of thousand of people. Because, I got a your stick that you threw from on the stage. It happened when Monday 14th June, 1982.

Your performance was amazed at me. I'm so happy about it. The sound of you really knocks my heart out. Of course, your drumming is best for me. I want to become a drummer just like you. I can play the drum a little. I'm strong and husky. Because I have played tennis for several years.

Yuki concludes with a wonderful diagram of Rick flying through the air towards a Premier drumkit sat astride a drumstick.

The band took to wearing kamikaze headbands for the duration of the second of their three tours, without really understanding what they meant. However, they came close to finding out on their return flight. Bruce and Rick rarely had problems getting along together, but, making their way back to Los Angeles from Tokyo to film a couple of TV shows, they enjoyed easily their most fierce confrontation.

Long-haul airline flights had long been a bugbear to The Jam and pop stars the world over. In common with many of their peers, the band had discovered a highly imaginative way of numbing the boredom suffered on such occasions. Drinking, in moderately vast quantities, became the name of the game.

Everybody, crew and band included, had made good use of the in-flight bar. Particularly Bruce, who had managed to get himself barred for his indulgences. Being homicidally drunk, and faced with the proposition of receiving no more service from a conventional source, Bruce's mind clicked round on his possibilities. And there he spied a dozing Rick Buckler, his bottle of duty free vodka clutched to his chest.

The JAM

When Rick, who had passed out as much as fallen asleep, came to, he was more concerned about his missing vodka than the small fact that the aeroplane was coming in to land. Rick's already crimson eyes saw redder still when they located his bottle of vodka, empty, in the hands of one time friend Bruce Foxton.

His response was as immediate as his inebriation allowed. He staggered accusingly towards his rhythm partner and exchanged a few words. 'Something along the lines of "You bastard!"' prompts Rick. 'And I lunged at him'. Bruce responded in like, to the bemusement of fellow Jam travellers and the utter consternation of the air crew. Blows were exchanged, dulled only by the muscle sapping effects of alcohol, before they could be prised apart by sundry air crew and roadies and separated. They were promptly instructed to behave themselves.

And behave themselves they did, until at least five seconds later. Just as the wheels skidded across the runway, Bruce and Rick once more found themselves swapping punches. Somewhere, at the back of their frazzled minds, Bruce hated Rick for his unprovoked attack and Rick hated Bruce for the cowardly theft of his liquor. So they hit each other a few more times, before, almost like boxers pulled apart by the bell, they were restrained and sent to their seats once more.

A brief lull in the proceedings passed as they queued for the customs gate. At which time it occurred to both parties that a cessation in hostilities was premature, and now was as good a time as any to start hitting each other again. Which they did, with as much ferocity as they could muster. 'I hadn't finished yet', offers Rick, in explanation. 'Neither had I' concurs Bruce.

John Weller was frantic. 'He was scared stiff that if we

carried on we wouldn't be let through customs, and that me and Rick would be put straight back on a plane to England, or worse still, Japan. So he was shouting "For fuck's sake, just let's get into the country first, you can kick the shit out of each other afterwards."'

Separated into different cars, each party licked their wounds as they were transported to the hotel. However, reunification reminded Rick and Bruce of how aggrieved they were at the actions of the other. So, true to type, 'We started to hit each other again'.

Probably the greatest casualty was Bruce, who had just invested a considerable sum of money on a watch. Japan had recently introduced the annoying digital model which can tell you the time in five different continents, and both Bruce and John Weller had been unable to resist the temptation to purchase one. 'It was one of those stupid things which could tell you what the time was in Bombay. But of course I was dead proud of it' mourns Bruce. At least John Weller's had made it beyond American airspace. Perhaps, in addition to water, weather and pressure proofing, the Japanese technicians should seek to develop a model impervious to a drunken Buckler uppercut.

John Weller, typically, was still not impressed. He stamped up and down the hotel corridors for several hours muttering about how a three piece band could continue when two of their number were at each other's throats. Luckily for John, by the time Bruce and Rick sobered up the event had been practically forgotten. 'Until someone asked Bruce the time', notes Rick.

Things were rarely this fraught between them. In slightly happier times, Rick made the faux pas of presenting Bruce with a Christmas present; a bottle of bacardi, that being the tipple always requested on his rhythm partner's rider.

Bruce opened the cupboard at his house to reveal some 18 bottles of the stuff, which he had accumulated over the years. In fact, Bruce can still boast that at least one of them remains unopened.

Bruce was also capable of the odd self-confessed 'tantrum' in times of stress. Pouring a bottle of beer over the mixing desk during one gig being a good example. Sound man Bob Jeffries, normally the most unassuming of guys, started having kittens as the monitors, PA and amps dipped in and out. 'Well', admits Bruce, 'I could get a little out of hand at times. I certainly had my moments'.

There were, in fact, relatively few disputes between the band as a whole. Probably the most important factor was their domestic habits. Unlike many groups on the road, The Jam did not socialise with each other too much outside of their duties as band members. None of the band particularly keen to contact the others when they came off tour. 'It was a working relationship, though we did continue to have a lot of fun on the road. In the early days we were just friends down the pub, but when our domestic situation changed, so did our social lives'. By this point in their career the chance to spend a couple of weeks off with the missus was cherished. Which again, placed Paul's decision to take Gill with him on the tours in a different light.

In his defence, things were a little different for Paul. The pressures of songwriting were becoming practically his alone. At the same time he was becoming progressively more wary of interviews, particularly with the 'NME' whose burdensome psycho-analysis always called for explanations beyond the call of duty. Or record promotion anyway. An unhealthy 'paternal' relationship had been set in motion by writers of both the 'NME' and Melody Maker, which occasionally found Weller gagging under the weight of expectation. The fanaticism of The Jam's fan base also presented problems. Previously the band had been keen to talk to the audience after gigs, and made a point of allowing them in to watch sound checks. Such gestures were becoming logistical nightmares now. It got to the point where more and more kids turned up in the afternoon knowing they could get in free to take in The Jam's 'matinee' performance.

Many ticketless fans also learned that they could gain entry to the gig proper by hiding in the toilets after the sound check. On other occasions the band would lie and say that some of the kids were relatives to help them through security. However, these itinerant kids also served a purpose. 'I suppose having them around all the time helped vibe up the venue. It became more of an event and was a bit more fun than just hanging around all day waiting for the gig'. Many of the hard-core fanatics became familiar faces, and the band still relished the opportunity of speaking to their audiences whenever possible.

Paul had managed to temper his hatred of touring the US somewhat, albeit by indulging in the delights of Mickey, Donald and Goofy. Bruce made the pilgrimage to Disneyland with him, though the latter declined to wear his Mickey Mouse ears through customs, which Paul decided was the appropriate course of action. 'As if drunken rock 'n' rollers passing through the gates of the airport terminal weren't enough to attract attention anyway'.

Similarly in Japan during their first tour there, Paul did his best to infuriate customs officials. He pulled out his biggest and brightest 'I Love Paul McCartney' badge. Which might not have seemed too anarchic, had the former Beatle not been arrested a few short months previously for marijuana possession. 'I think Paul was trying to make a point', adds Bruce, 'but I don't think anyone took any notice whatsoever'.

The JAM

Touring abroad was never simply fun and games. Rick and Bruce were about to become victims of the popular Los Angeles tourist sport of mugging before 'minder' Kenny Wheeler intervened. Rick in particular remembers having his back edged firmly back to the window of a nearby shop while the matter was resolved. Eventually it transpired that Kenny's cockney accent had seen the attempted assailants reliving the myths of the Kray Twins, and they subsequently thought better of their actions. 'Or perhaps Kenny's eighteen stone frame might also have influenced them' is Bruce's considered opinion.

CHAPTER NINE

The Bitterest Pill

The early stages of 1982 were dominated by the recording of their sixth album. Sessions had begun in December of the previous year at Air Studios in Oxford Street. Two days after its release they played a secret gig in Guildford on March the 6th to celebrate John and Ann Weller's Silver Wedding Anniversary. Things had come full circle in many ways, the band had built their early reputation on weddings, parties, bar mitzvahs and the like...But this one was a little special.

Another double a-sider returned them to the number one spot. Coupling 'A Town Called Malice' with 'Precious' came close to squandering your assets. Both songs brought mainstream dance-floor approval to the band for the first time. Lyrically Weller was less happy with 'Malice's attempt to incorporate the Motown rhythm - he himself compared it less favourably with Madness' 'Embarrassment'. 'Precious', meanwhile, was a classy stab at white funk with Weller throwing himself wholeheartedly in to the soaring vocals. 'Top Of The Pops' invited them to appear playing both songs back to back. It was the first time such a thing had happened since the Beatles' achieved the same feat with 'Day Tripper'/'We Can Work It Out'. 'It felt like the establishment was finally tipping its

The JAM

hat to us. On that level, it probably meant more to us than it did to Aunty Beeb'.

Polydor quickly learned that The Jam's enormous fan base would buy everything with their name on it on the week of release. Hence they decided on the marketing ploy of releasing a more limited initial batch to keep The Jam's records at the top of the charts for as long as possible.

The album which housed the double-headed single was close to spiritual in conception. Weller was making statements in the press about calls for unity, and the 'special gift each of us are born with'. It might unkindly be described as his nouveau hippy phase. A grand scheme it was too, but one which was not always flattered by the execution. Speaking on the musical slant of 'The Gift', Weller was keen for the work not to be stereotyped as derivative. The incorporation of black music styles was obvious to everyone. It signalled a change in musical direction which would characterise his subsequent recordings with the Style Council. After the flaws in 'Sound Affects' he was also hyped up to produce the ultimate Jam album. The year taken out of the band's schedule prior to recording was a big clue to Weller's commitment to this end.

'The Gift' saw The Jam dispense with Vic Coppersmith Heaven for the first time, with engineer Pete Wilson stepping up to full production duties. 'Pete had been working with Paul on demos and I think Paul preferred that more instant approach, that he wouldn't get with Vic. It gave him more of a free hand, and helped bring out the live sound he'd been talking to us about. From our point of view we thought it was the right time to make a break, because apart from anything else each of us knew what we were doing in the studio now', recounts Rick. 'From my point of view', adds Bruce, 'we were at the stage where all we needed was a good sound engineer rather than a producer'.

Four London shows around this time revealed an increased awareness of the band's Motown roots, not just with 'A Town Called Malice' but covers of Chairman Of The Board's 'Give Me Just A Little More Time' and Smokey Robinson tunes. The Jam now had their own 'brass' section with Keith Thomas and Steve Nichol, who had joined in time for the London CND shows. They were inducted in to The Jam touring jamboree by taking the stage in Japan unaware that the saxophone had been lined with talcum powder. Recalls Rick, 'I don't remember him finding that very funny, as he was very precious about his instrument'.

The passion for experimentation occasionally outstripped The Jam's abilities. 'The Planners Dream Gone Wrong' was the best example of this - pseudo calypso on which Weller candidly confessed, they were out of their league. The cinematic title had shades of the 'Creature From The Black Lagoon' as Weller launched in to a predictable indictment of unfeeling 50s social policy.

'Ghosts' was a typical mini-morality play, encased in a so-so soul ballad, while 'Happy Together' was a light-hearted love song taken directly from Weller's own relationship. Of considerable merit is the European released single 'Just Who Is the 5 o'clock Hero'. Huge import purchases raised the song, like 'That's Entertainment' before it, straight in to the UK charts. It celebrates the normality of working class life; Weller using the song to reinstate the dignity of working men and women. It is charmingly reminiscent of the scene in 'The Magnificent Seven' where one of the desperadoes takes a peasant child over his knee for suggesting his parents are cowards.

'Transglobal Express' was comfortably the most experimental track. It implicitly stressed the need for communication and contact which Weller was trying to articulate to the press. Whether unconsciously or not, his lyrics were moving from the arena of questions to solutions. He spoke of several feelings he wanted to get across with the song (political rally, dub, new Grandmaster Flash techniques). Its eclecticism is aided and abetted by the lyrical scope which takes in Weller's feelings on touring various parts of the country. It contrasts nicely with 'Running On The Spot', a put down of the tunnel vision punk class of 1982

'Carnation' once more concerned a semi-religious search for meaning in struggle, which harked back to 'Man In The Corner Shop'. Bruce's songwriting role had been reduced to contributing instrumentals by this point, though his 'Circus' is more than simply light relief. This grand little jig is Bruce's most effective album track after the orchestral treatment afforded 'Smithers-Jones' on 'Setting Sons'.

Weller's retrospective attitude to the album seemed to indicate that he thought its lapses confirmed The Jam had exhausted their own musical conventions. That the band had been overtaken by his personal musical vision. Not surprisingly, Bruce and Rick do not share that opinion. 'We thought we'd done a good job on the album. Obviously Paul was heading off in a new direction, but there was nothing that he was writing then or subsequently that we didn't think we could have turned our hand to'.

On one occasion during the recording sessions for the album, Rick remembers having to leave early when Lesley telephoned the studio to say that his pipes had burst. Water was flooding through every room of his house and Rick had to pack up his sticks and motor through town. The imperative nature of Rick's exit was lost on Paul, who continued to moan about Rick being tied to the capitalist money making machine and being a slave to the banks. Rick's mind however, was purely on his carpets, upholstery, and having to find somewhere to sleep that night.

"SORRY LADS" I THOUGHT IT WAS SUIT DAY

GOING FOR IT

GONE FOR IT

PAUL DEEP IN THOUGHT

164

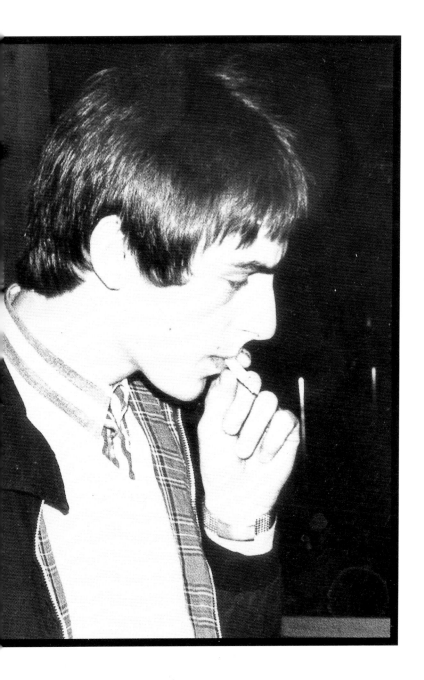

THE BIG TIME! - BLUE NUN & ONE ROOM

HAS ANYONE SEEN PAUL

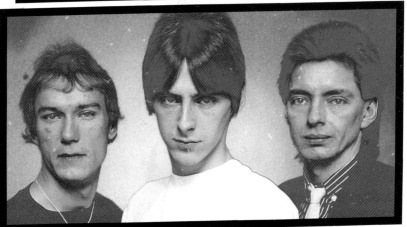

PROMO CLASSICS!

ON THE ROOF OF BATTERSEA POWER STATION

NAME EM!

PAUL AT WORK

I'LL FIND MY WAY OUT SOON

CAKE AND CANDLES FOR PAUL'S BIRTHDAY

THE TUBE STUDIOS, NEWCASTLE

PAUL "WOT A LOT OF PLECTRUMS" WELLER

ME TRUSS HAS BROKE

ON TV AGAIN

174

MIRROR, MIRROR ON THE WALL......

WHICH BIT DO I BLOW DOWN

The Jam

On the customary trek to support 'The Gift', dubbed the 'Trans-Global Unity Express' tour, Paul was somewhat distressed at seeing his audience chant for The Jam all the way through the support act's set. 'I think that definitely made him wonder about whether or not he was getting through to people. We didn't like it either, because it meant that your audience wasn't actually listening to what you were saying, or what we were about. It made us feel like just another pop band with screaming fans.'

March 1982 brought Rick Buckler face to face with the sheer magnitude of The Jam's following on that same tour. Performing at the Brighton Conference Centre, the band were staying at the Grand Hotel next door. A small, secret entrance was available to celebrities who could discreetly move from their hotel to the venue. Rick, tagging along behind idly one evening, suddenly found himself confronted by a locked door. Evidently the guard had presumed everybody to be safely ensconced in the building and subsequently locked the door. Rick banged away for a good ten minutes trying to raise the alarm, before he realised that there was no way he was going to make himself heard. With gig time approaching, he was forced to return to the hotel and walk round. However, as soon as he reached the alleyway he saw some fans waiting there, and decided to nip round the front and down the hill to the venue.

Not wishing to cause any undue alarm, Rick moseyed down the road without daring to look over his shoulder. However, footsteps behind him confirmed the presence of a hundred or so Jam fans curious to ascertain his identity. Hearing the whisper turn from "Is it?" to "It is!", Rick tried to subtly increase his pace. The crowd gathering behind him, in the style of the best Buster Keaton sketch, increased their pace in sympathy. Rick broke into a brisk walk, trot, and finally a sprint for the doors of the venue.

The JAM

Rick landed there a few short seconds before his pursuers. However, his next obstacle was a security man who wasn't about to let anyone in. "I'm not opening the doors yet" he mouthed to the crowd, pointing to his watch, as Rick was compressed against the door. Knocking again, Rick managed to persuade his tormentor to open the door a crack. However, the strain of doing so left him breathless, and unable to reply in time to the security guard's sour "Have you got a ticket then?". Rick, incredulous, finally managed a return volley of, "No, I haven't got a fucking ticket!". Before he could go on to add that he really shouldn't need a ticket, the guard officiously declared "Right, you're not coming in then!". It took Rick a good five minutes of claustrophobic interrogation to convince the doorman of his status. In the end the fans themselves joined in: 'They were all going "Let him in, he's The Jam's drummer". They realised if they didn't get me in, then there wouldn't be a gig for them to go to.'

The event brought two responses. The first was hilarity at the situation. However, something else also occurred to Rick. 'Well, in a sense it felt like it didn't really matter what happened to me. They'd got Paul in the venue, and I was just the drummer. I know it sounds paranoid, but I found out later that nobody had made any attempt to find me. They didn't even know I'd gone'.

It was still Paul who suffered from the worst excesses of fandom. On one occasion his sartorial elegance nearly cost him his life. Having taken to wearing the long, college scarf featured in many latter day photo sessions, he had probably never considered the garment a possible lethal weapon. Stepping out of a doorway in Newcastle, two enthusiastic fans made a grab for the scarf from either side of him. Consequently Paul found the breath being sucked out of him as he tried to ward off his admirers. It was, possibly, a neat analogy for his state of mind.

By this stage in their career, the band were so popular that they were fair game for fans before or after gigs. And The Jam's fan base was nothing if not resourceful. They had long since discovered that by ringing around hotels in a given city, and asking if "Mr Weller, Foxton, or Buckler" was staying there, they could determine the location of their heroes. So the band developed pseudonyms for touring. 'Unfortunately', recalls Rick, 'It only occurred to us later that we hadn't given one for John Weller. Which was pretty stupid really cos the fans sussed straight away.'

Various ploys and stratagems were developed to enable the band to avoid mobbing after gigs. When they discovered that they were being followed from the venue to their hotel by fans in cars, they hit upon parking the tour van out front, and escaping out the back in promoter Tim Parson's three-litre Capri. 'But they soon sussed that out. I remember one venue we were literally stuck in the dressing room for hours waiting for the crowds to disperse. It was like being under siege'.

Other brushes with fandom were less fraught. Roger Pilling, the band's old friend from the days of illicit smoking in the toilets of Sheerwater High, turned up from nowhere at one gig. Paul joined him for a drink. A nervous fan walked over to ask him for his autograph. Paul signed his scrap of paper, before passing it over to Roger who did likewise. Out of the corner of their eyes they saw the fan slope off to his chair. For a full five minutes he kept looking up, mystified, at the tall ginger frame of Mr Pilling. Then he would look back down at the names on his piece of paper. Eventually he tore the sheet of paper in half and threw one of the names away. We can only presume the discarded autograph was that of Roger Pilling.

The European stretch of the tour saw the band taking in

The JAM

Sweden, Denmark, Holland, France and Belgium. For security man Joe Awome, however, his tour nearly began and ended in Scandinavia. During their date at the Isstadion in Stockholm, one of the local punks had decided to cause a bit of mayhem. The Jam security guards were always well briefed on their conduct towards the fans, and would calm trouble-makers down rather than eject them. 'This guy', recalls Rick 'was just bent on ruining everyone else's evening. So Joe Awome chucked him out'.

Unfortunately for him, he happened to be chanced upon by some local youths who presumably decided his manner of dress indicated that he warranted a good kicking. Which he promptly received. 'So he rang the police' continues Rick, 'and told them it was down to The Jam and our security. So they arrested Joe and threw him into this totally over the top, high security jail. And they wouldn't let him go. And of course, we only had another day before we left the country. So for a while there it was pretty touch and go whether we'd have to desert him'. Luckily for Joe and the rest of the entourage, a witness came forward and confirmed Joe's innocence just in time.

Stationed in New York in May, The Jam were preparing to play a gig at the Ritz the day after Paul's birthday. Rick had come up with an inspired idea for a present. Being on the books of Premier, and all the sponsorship freebies that involved, Rick had managed to coax a second kit out of them. Paul was forever mucking about with Rick's stage set-up, and bemoaning the fact that he didn't have one of his own. However, there was no way Rick was going to go through the hassle of transporting the thing to America just so that he could present it on the day. Instead he took several pictures of it once it was set up back in Blighty, and placed the photo in a card and signed it with love from Rick.

The Jam

Paul was having a small do in the bar, while Rick handed over the card and announced that the kit was back in London waiting for him. Unfortunately Paul, a little the worse for wear, misunderstood completely. He thought Rick had struck upon the brilliant scheme of simply giving him a photograph of a drum kit, and was suitably unimpressed. Rick was similarly aggrieved, and spent the rest of the evening over the other side of the bar with a serious bottom-lip on him. 'Well, you can imagine how chuffed I was about that'.

Later in the evening, possibly through the efforts of John Weller, Paul realised exactly what had happened. It was, in fact, a real drum kit and all his own. Consequently he trooped straight up to Rick's hotel room and knocked on the door, visibly better pleased than he had been.

It was common practice for the band to invite their families up for the last London show of the UK tour. However, in the summer of 1982, with a mid-tour slot in Jersey booked, it was decided to go to the expense of shipping all their family and friends out for a couple of days of sun at the band's expense. Designed to be just a little bit special, it was a happy time for everyone in the band. 'Basically it just seemed a good opportunity to have a bit of a knees-up'. It was also, to all intents and purposes, the calm before the storm.

The release of 'Bitterest Pill' was less than encouraging, a deliberately trite love song which many reviewers were taken in by. Whether or not it was a joke couldn't disguise the fact that it was The Jam's worst single for some time. Fittingly, the melancholic lyrics to the song served as a nice analogy for the internal politics of the band. By the time of its release Weller had already told Foxton and Buckler of his decision to quit.

The JAM

In June Paul called a meeting with Bruce and Rick at Marcus studios where they were about to record 'The Bitterest Pill'. What he had to say took their breath away, as well as their livelihood. It was the end of the road for The Jam.

Bruce and Rick struggled to absorb the news. One of the first options offered to him was to take a break, a year off or more if he was finding it difficult. But Paul was adamant; he was leaving. Rick and Bruce could not even contemplate continuing without Paul. To all intents and purposes the group's main songwriter, they each felt that had one of them left before this point, that too would have meant the end. 'I suppose that was like an unspoken thing, a gentleman's agreement'.

Touring Japan earlier in the year there had been a sense of something amiss in the ranks. Neither Bruce nor Rick could quite put their finger on what it was. If anything, they reckoned it was being caused by the problems Paul was experiencing in his relationship with Gill. 'They hadn't been getting on at all well and we sort of put it down to that'. However, they would not have long to wait to discover the reason for Paul's mood.

Paul had reflected on the future of the band during a two week Italian holiday with Gill during the summer of 1982. The decision was totally unilateral. John Weller was similarly non-plussed by his son's actions. After all, the band had not cracked America yet, and Paul's father maintained a dream of seeing his son selling-out Madison Square Gardens.

Paul had spoken to them of wishing to escape the treadmill of single - album- tour imposed on a successful rock band. Bruce and Rick sympathised with the pressure of having to write to order and being ruled by a contract. But his deci-

The JAM

sion to defect almost immediately to the Style Council, who would operate on very much the same level, left a bitter aftertaste. Most importantly, perhaps, Bruce and Rick felt there was genuine creative mileage left in The Jam. To this day they still believe the band could have continued to progress and grow for at least another two albums.

Devastated by the news, Rick called in to see Lesley who was working behind a bar. There weren't too many people in the pub, so Rick gently leant across the bar and whispered 'Look, don't tell *anybody*, but the band is finishing'. Feeling distraught and thoroughly empty, Rick walked home and sat staring at a wall for a couple of hours. He was unable to find it within himself to believe it was happening. 'I suppose I was in shock really.'

Bruce chose to get drunk. When Pat arrived home from work (she had a job at CBS at the time), he spilled out what had happened. She helped him resolve that "something would turn up". The rest is clouded in the mists of massive intoxication.

The worst scenario had come true for Rick and Bruce. Neither really had an alternative career, and they had expected the band's demise to come when they weren't getting on any more, or had stopped being successful. Neither of these scenarios applied. 'I think we'd have been able to understand it better then. But not when everything was going so well'.

The band completed the sessions for 'The Bitterest Pill', which they remember, ironically enough, as being musically excellent. Both Bruce and Rick half expected Paul to change his mind. They reasoned that Paul had been going through a bad patch with Gill, and out of the trio he came in for most pressure in terms of songwriting and promotional duties.

So initially, despite Paul's statement, they still couldn't believe the situation was that clear cut. But as the year wore on, hope diminished. Trying to keep the secret from the music press was difficult, and inevitably it slipped out before they could announce it officially. A hurried statement on October 30 1982 carried the news to the nation. Bruce and Rick began to realise it really was all over.

But they had to grit their teeth. The video for 'Bitterest Pill' proved particularly galling, and one of the most obvious examples of the way the wind had changed in The Jam camp. 'Paul had all his various mates roped in', and the rest of the band were beginning to feel like entirely secondary characters. The girl kissed on the video was in fact Lee Kavanagh, who sang on Department S' 'Is Vic There' single. Not, as many people presumed, Gill. Paul had been introduced to Lee by the band's singer Vaughan Toulouse. Toulouse also appeared on the single's cover and worked with Paul again before sadly dying of AIDS. The vocalist on the actual duet sequence was Jenny McKeown, of the Belles Stars.

Bruce in particular wasn't too delighted at this turn of events: 'It was just becoming the Paul Weller show, with all his cronies. We'd never really liked any sort of video where we had to act, because we weren't very good at that sort of thing. Yet here we were waiting around for absolutely ages to get the filming done, and we were being made to hang around all day and into the early hours of the morning. In the end I just thought stuff this and drove home. I don't think anything was ever said about it afterwards, it was probably just put down as Bruce having another of his moods.'

The irritatingly small scene that Rick and Bruce had been hanging around to complete was simply a shot of their backs. As the video had to be completed in one day, A&R man Dennis Munday manages a decent impersonation of the Foxton flank in the final sequence.

In the interim the band had the distraction of the final, 'Oh no, not another Tour' tour. Playing out live pushed the thought of the band's dissolution to the back of their minds, and the trek was completed in its entirety prior to the announcement of the split. Paul wasn't helped by a bout of shingles, but generally the band agree that the tour was their best for some time. Over the last couple of years Paul's boredom with the live routine was becoming more and more evident. But, with his future resolved, 'he actually seemed to be enjoying himself again', notes Bruce. The tour also saw the introduction of backing vocalists Afrodiziac (featuring later Soul II Soul contributor and solo artist Caron Wheeler) and keyboard player Jimmy Telford.

The band also opened up the first series of 'The Tube', one of rock's more successful attempts to adopt the cathode ray. Of all The Jam's television appearances this one, which took place on the 5th of November 1982, was arguably the most important.

The announcement of the split had become public knowledge just a few days previously. The programme began with Paul discussing his new projects and plans for the future, before a mini-length Jam concert was broadcast. Featuring 'Ghosts', 'In The Crowd', 'Town Called Malice', 'The Modern World', 'Move On Up', 'The Great Depression' and 'Precious'. It was an amiable and representative selection of the modern Jam sound. For many it would be the closest they would get to seeing the band live, and an adequate demonstration of their verve and power on stage. However, there were few smiles on stage; both Rick and Bruce looking understandably drawn and uneasy.

The JAM

'Beat Surrender' was an impressive final vinyl outpouring. It saw Weller paraphrase the Bible: 'As it was in the beginning, so shall it be in the end, The bullshit is bullshit, just goes by different names.' But in terms of epitaphs, it is worth noting the one penned by Pete Townshend in Time Out. Amongst other things he stated: 'I have never come across another artist or writer so afraid of appearing hypocritical'. The Jam had long since turned down the offer of supporting their heroes.

The double-pack single which was issued by Polydor boasted covers of 'Stoned Out Of My Mind' (Chi-Lites) and 'Move On Up' (Curtis Mayfield). These were certainly OK, but it was the standard issue b-side cut 'Shopping' which stole the show. Its jazzy tones pre-empted the Style Council and featured powerhouse drumming from Buckler - avec brushes naturally.

A final appearance on 'Top Of The Pops' proved to be another strange ordeal. After rehearsing and recording, the band trooped off. Despite being at number one, there was none of the usual high spirits with the band's death knell still ringing in their ears. Bruce found himself propping up the bar on his tod, trying to work out how and why the bottom had just fallen out of his world.

Going to the toilet, he remembered a small ball of cannabis resin he had been handed by one of the road crew. Now Bruce was probably the least disposed to such substances within the band. 'After all, I didn't even smoke, and I couldn't 'roll up' to save my life'. So, depressed by the turn of events taking place around him, Bruce decided he might cheer himself up a little if he swallowed the lump.

Which turned out to be an ill-advised move. Bruce spent the rest of the evening stumbling through BBC towers hallucinating, desperately trying to find someone he knew.

The Jam

And by the time he did happen across some friendly faces, they took great delight in informing him that his present condition was his own silly fault. Bruce was too confused to accept the wisdom of these words, concentrating instead on which stretch of wall was the ceiling, and which was the floor.

The farewell 'Beat Surrender' tour was not the happy farewell it might have been. Rick even noticed a subdued anger in the audience which matched their own resentment. When fans jostled backstage to ask Rick and Bruce why they were splitting up the most important thing in the world to them, neither had an answer.

The final series of gigs at Wembley (though the very last one would take place at Brighton) began with 'Hello and welcome to the Red Cow' and closed with 'Don't wanna get too sentimental or anything....but thanks for the last six years'. The Jam had communicated with sufficient emotive power over their life-span to make further words unnecessary. Except, perhaps, within the band itself.

The impact of playing their songs for the last time was powerful enough, as was seeing the fans for a final time. 'But we also felt a lot of bitterness. Having worked for so many years to achieve this level of popularity, we didn't really want to throw in the towel at the height of our careers. Not just the five years we had been professional, but for five before that we had been more than just a band. For us Paul's decision didn't add up at all'.

To rub salt in to the wound, the addition of a final date at Brighton for monetary reasons did not sit happily. If it had to finish, then both Bruce and Rick wanted the curtain to be called at the Guildford show; a much more natural conclusion to the band's history. Packing out Wembley for five successive nights might have been lucrative, but it 'never felt natural'. Apart from the additional Wembley and Brighton dates, most of the tour had already been pencilled in prior to the split, so there was limited justification in calling it a 'Farewell Tour'.

That final set at Brighton was awkward and uncomfortable. It never really gelled and provided something of an anti-climax to band and audience alike. The morning after Bruce woke up feeling utterly empty. 'Suddenly there was no camaraderie anymore, no "Great tour, see you again in four weeks". None of that was going to happen ever again'.

Bruce had been in a desperate state throughout the tour. Unlike Rick or Paul, who are of a much less fretful nature, he simply wasn't able to truly accept the situation. Staying at the Grand on that final night was merely the icing on a particularly unhappy cake.

In truth, Bruce nearly didn't make it as far as the final round of gigs. Devastated by Paul's decision to quit, he wasn't sure if he'd be able to cope with a last stint. John Weller stepped in to try and persuade him, and he was talked round quite quickly. 'I suppose you could say I did it for selfish reasons. My whole career had been pulled from under my feet, and a few extra dates meant some financial security for me and Pat'.

Even the Christmas Party, which the band had held for several years, was a low-key affair. Held at the Fulham Greyhound, December 19th 1982 saw a muted event held under the premise of saying thank you and goodbye to all their friends and employees. Held eight days after the farewell gig, there had been no contact between Paul and the other members of the band and they found the party effectively 'sectioned off'. Usually there was a buzz created by the fawning industry types who attended such events. However, with no more Jam on the horizon the vultures had flown. Which left several mutual friends, and three factions of Paul's mates, Rick's mates and Bruce's mates in huddles. 'It was more like a wake than a party'.

The band had only really gone to pick up their 'present' from Polydor. Which was a mistake really, as such gifts had become increasingly naïf, seemingly in inverse proportion to the band's success. And now The Jam were splitting up they really didn't have to bother. In previous years the band had collected TV's, videos, Cartier watches and the like. In 1982 Rick and Bruce left the Fulham Greyhound with a solid silver rhinoceros. One each.

It may have been worth a few bob, but at the time Bruce merely wanted to shove it up Paul's backside. 'Sideways'.

It was small consolation that Bruce and Rick now had time to assess just how big The Jam's impact was. The most consistently successful UK singles partnership since the Beatles, the accolade ranked merely as a nice personal achievement in the light of the band's break-up. Nobody in the band had ever been that affected by trinkets of this type.

'The sight of some 10,000 people queuing for our gig at Decsides Leisure Centre was what put it across to me', recalls Rick. 'It really did take me a while to realise that they weren't queuing for free milk or something, but they had all actually come to see us'. To physically witness a crowd of those proportions was far more tangible than Brian Morrison, The Jam's publisher, coming to the'Top Of The Pops'studio and informing the band that they had sold 30,000 records that day.

The Jam story was wrapped up in an official format with Paulo Hewitt's authorised biography, 'A Beat Concerto'. Paulo, a long-time friend of Paul Weller's, was undoubtedly too close to his subject to deal with it with objectivity. No more than a single hour was spent with Bruce and Rick combined, and thus the mythology of The Jam continued to be that promoted by the Weller camp. It went through Paul's publishing company, and it reflected a quite singular perspective on the group. 'The statement on the back cover of the book saying that the text leaves nothing else to be said on its subject still rankles with us. Factually it was severely flawed, even down to calling Bruce's old band Zita. The first we saw of any of it was when it was serialised in the Record Mirror'.

More recently, Bruce and Rick have continued to have their run-ins with Paul's 'Best Mate'. Especially when Paulo compiled the sleeve notes for the 'Extras' set. 'Not only did they have the same slant as the book, which we obviously hated, but he even had the cheek to deliver the "Me and Paul were walking down the street" anecdote again. He may well have had the honour of walking down the street with Paul but that had nothing to do with the recordings on the release. That applied to a date far in advance of when they were recorded'. When Bruce and Rick saw proofs and objected, Paulo simply stated that he was not about to amend them because of what they said. It is this self-imposed "fourth Jam member" mentality that Bruce and Rick find abhorrent. 'After all, over several hundred gigs neither of us can remember one where he appeared on stage with us'.

Polydor cashed in with two worthwhile albums. A token live affair, 'Dig The New Breed', was doomed never to catch the band's mesmeric energy, but it came respectably close. It was, in truth, the classic contract-filler ('we still owed Polydor an album and Paul was in no mood to record any new songs'). For the release each member was asked to individually sift through a mountain of live tapes to select suitable candidates. However, the project did

The JAM

allow them the chance to pen their own epitaph to their career; the closest they came following the 'Beat Concerto' frustrations. A huge number of tracks were half-mixed before final mixing took place on the selected songs. However, Paul and Pete Wilson effectively had the final say, after Paul had purchased what was originally Polydor's studio off them.

They also had the final say over 'Snap!', an excellent double album of prime Jam. With sleeve notes cobbled together from the omniscient Paulo Hewitt and his book, it was nevertheless a tremendous package. The track selection is particularly commendable, with few essential Jam compositions missed out.

The water was definitely muddied, however, by 1991's shoddy 'Greatest Hits' package. Polydor's string-a-long a singles compilation sounded good ('It also looked good perched on the top of the charts after all these years') but the presentation was reprehensible. This time the 'sleeve notes' were composed of grammatically ambivalent, juvenile clichés. Among a gamut of sins they described 'Tube Station' as a ballad....'Yeah, we couldn't believe it either' nods Rick. It still sold 250,000 copies.

Those responsible at the record company went some way towards atonement with 'Extras', a handsome rummage through The Jam's back pages. It is comprised principally of solo demos dating from the 'Setting Sons'/'Sound Affects' period, which provide handy work-in-progress hints for the avid Weller watcher. There are also a couple of unreleased numbers and a series of long deleted b-sides. And if The Jam were a great singles band many of these were at least the equal of their flips.

Highlights include a pre-Style Council recording of 'A Solid Bond In Your Heart' (which was to have been the final single at one point), and the previously mentioned 'No One In The World'. Its also very handy to be able to listen through tracks like 'Butterfly Collector' and 'Dreams Of Children' without digging through the singles racks time and again.

Following the announcement of their split Polydor re-released all the bands singles in their original sleeves, leading to The Jam having no less than thirteen singles in the Top Hundred simultaneously. Weller's decision brought new lustre to the term 'going out on top', even if it wasn't much consolation to two thirds of the band. The Jam were saluted as one of the great singles bands, a tribute savoured by Weller: 'I've always been in to singles, and with the rising cost of LPs singles are going to be the future of the record anyway'. Admirable sentiments from Paul, but you can't be right all the time. Even if you are a spokesman for a generation.

CHAPTER TEN

Music For The Last Couple

Paul defected to the Style Council with dizzying speed. Over several years he would release a succession of records to steadily diminishing financial and artistic returns. The 'blue-eyed soul' trick only ever clicked very occasionally. As David Sinclair succinctly states in his book 'Rock CD': '(The Style Council were) a group who virtually redefined the concept of carrying on to the point of meaninglessness, and indeed some distance beyond'. His new adventures held little appeal for either Bruce or Rick: 'It wasn't that we thought it wasn't any good, it was more that the music was just not our style. It just wasn't the sort of thing we enjoyed listening to'. The Style Council split in 1990 after Polydor rejected their latest album.

To be fair to Paul, he has gone a long way towards redeeming himself via his current solo career, which followed on from his time in the Paul Weller Movement. Ironically, his current solo repertoire now forms part of a determined effort to crack the resistance of his old bogey man: the USA.

Having seen Paul move straight on to the Style Council, Bruce and Rick each elected to move quickly to other projects to keep their careers moving. Time UK evolved out of jamming sessions held almost immediately following the split. Rick contacted Jimmy Edwards, who was also at Polydor, who was trying to make his name as a songwriter rather than a performer. However, his actions under the latter guise had included a version of 'In The City'.

Time UK was drawn together quite swiftly. Rick was keen not to 'sit on my arse', and by March 1983 they were playing live. Members of the band included several good musicians, notably Danny Kustow (ex-Tom Robinson Band) on guitar, Martin Gordon (ex-Radio Stars) on bass and Nick South (ex-of everyone from Yoko Ono to Steve Marriot's All Stars). Intriguingly, Gordon can boast of having once been sacked from Sparks because he refused to use a Fender Precision bass - opting instead for his favoured Rickenbacker. Shades of Paul and Bruce?. However, the lack of proper management confined the outfit to short record deals that failed to lead them anywhere.

Bruce, meanwhile, very nearly forged a link with Jake Burns (ex-Stiff Little Fingers) prior to his inclusion in that band proper. Just as The Jam had split, the career of the Irish punk/pop outfit was put on hold too. Bruce recorded some songs with Jake immediately prior to the latter kick starting his Big Wheel outfit. Demos which never saw the light of day were recorded amid a couple of personnel changes.

Bruce admits that at this point 'I was panicking a little'. Desperate not to have too long a break in his career, he jumped at the opportunity of working on these sessions to maintain his profile. The outfit was shaping up reasonably well, but then the phone call from Jam publisher Brian Morrison came through. Brian talked Bruce in to pulling his own band together. 'Brian was a fairly typical publishing man', notes Bruce, 'ten foot cigar and a natty pin stripe suit job'. His "I'll get you a deal my boy" overtures were impossible to resist.

'It might have been a better idea to stick with what I was doing with Jake, in retrospect. That might have worked out well. I was talked into it by Brian, but I suppose I didn't really need that much talking into it because I wanted to get a record deal again and that was almost on the table'.

Bruce went out to buy himself a drum machine and a keyboard to make himself a stand-alone musical unit. By mid-1983 he had a contract with Arista Records. He was aware that this was wholly due to the record company's belief that they would be able to shift 50,000 units on his connection to The Jam alone: 'I wasn't that naive'. Brian Morrison had a number of musical contacts and through these a full touring/recording outfit was put together. An initial single 'Freak' was released and actually charted at Number 22, which proved quite encouraging. However, the panic which followed The Jam's collapse was still bubbling away beneath the surface. Bruce was attempting to manage himself, believing he might as well have total control over his destiny. It was a disaster. 'I totally underestimated the time involved in being the principal songwriter, managing your own finances and booking tour dates'.

The songwriting evidently suffered. Bruce reflects on his only solo album as being 'a half-baked affair, with too many rushed efforts and a lack of quality control'. He fully expected Arista to come back to him and say that several of the tracks were not good enough, just as Chris Parry had done in his days with The Jam. But presumably on the strength of Bruce's connection to that outfit, Arista seemed quite happy to merely accept what was being given to them. 'A manager or other third party might have helped, just to bounce ideas off or get some feedback.' Unaided, Bruce was destined to come unstuck.

Bruce was subsequently signed up to EMI as a songwriter for about a year, and managed one release on that label. But his chart success dwindled rapidly and with it his solo career.

A couple of years later, when any idea of a solo career had been knocked on the head by Bruce, he met up once more with his former rhythm partner Rick. Together they formed Sharp, alongside Jimmy Edwards and an American record manager, Mark Johnson. They recorded a solitary indie single. However, the whole thing was studio based and once again condemned to early failure by inadequate management. There was also the consideration of being perceived as the 'new Jam', 'which we didn't really want'.

Another of Bruce's adventures involved drummer Steve Jones (ex-UK Subs), who had also bashed the skins during his solo venture. The One Hundred Men actually lasted some three of four years, and the band came quite close to actually sewing up a deal. Gus Dudgeon, noted for his early work with Elton John, acted as producer at one point, and various 'names' in the industry were apparently monitoring their progress. However, ultimately the band would miss the boat, becoming another near-miss for Bruce. 'I had to give it a fair run before I realised it was probably time to call it a day'.

Rick had moved on to running his own studio in London for three years. Unfortunately, he would come unstuck financially and eventually lose his house over the losses. However, while there he hooked up with the Highliners, mostly looking after their management. When the drummer left, Rick stepped in on a temporary basis. He had found the band a deal with Razor in London. However, first he had to disentangle them from a contract with John Curd of ABC Records. The Highliners had recorded an album in Wales and the studio refused to release the tapes when Curd neglected to pay the bill.

Once more, Bruce returned to working with Rick in a new project, Built Like Stone, whose life-span was about a year this time. Described as vaguely "Psychedelic Furs-like", the other members of the band included two inexperienced London lads. They had found management this time, and the plan was to record a CD with a few tracks to get airplay. The two guys involved, one a distributor, one an entrepreneur, unfortunately fell on hard times. Once more it all fell away. The prospect of having to finance more demos, off their own back, and go round the circuit of record companies once more, proved too much for Rick. Bruce was prepared to hang in there a little longer, but once Rick made his position clear that was that. 'You've got to be able to say I draw the line here, otherwise, you'll spend the rest of your life going round in circles'.

Rick had recorded some of the initial demos for Big Country before the demise of The Jam. More recently he produced for the Family Cat. Bruce went on to work with the Rhythm Sisters, a pop funk outfit with two female vocalists and two guitarists. But eventually he would receive the call from Stiff Little Fingers again.

Where he remains to this day; happy to be part of a band once more, and having performed on both the recent studio albums. Rick's last live performances were with the Highliners (in Berlin, to be exact), though he has pro-grammed drums for a new age album with a friend to earn a crust. He is currently more than happy running his own, modestly successful, furniture restoration business.

Of course, whatever the respective solo efforts of Paul, Rick and Bruce, there will always remain speculation at the pos-sibility of a Jam reunion. 'Paul has clearly changed his opinion on some of the songs he wrote ten years ago, though it is apparent that more and more of his Jam work has resurfaced on his solo tours'. It may surprise many to note that Bruce and Rick are not as readily disposed to a reformation as might be assumed.

Although both felt sick about the way The Jam ended, neither has an appetite to reform a band simply to play their greatest hits around the country. 'The possible exception might have been 'Live Aid', though obviously Paul was already on stage with the Style Council'.

The other stumbling block is that, regretfully, since Paul split The Jam he hasn't spoken to either Rick or Bruce. Individually or collectively, Rick and Bruce have tried to contact Paul on several occasions. Not only on business grounds, but simply to stay in touch. But as far as Paul is concerned, the ties have been severed irrevocably. 'He's washed his hands of us'.

Particularly upsetting for Rick was a period when he would pop in to Stanhope Place, where Paul would be working in the Polygram studio. Paul refused to come out to see him, while Rick sat outside bored and angry. Neither Rick nor Bruce saw any point in trying to continue a musical relationship, but after all the years they spent together it took them some time to come to terms with the fact that Paul didn't want to know them anymore.

The last time Rick saw Paul was over a decade ago, in 1983 at one of Bruce's solo sets at Hammersmith. Rick came with Ray Simone from Time UK. Rick was standing at the back of the hall when he saw Paul coming over and said hello. 'Unfortunately, Ray, who is blind in one eye, came over and stood right in front of Paul. Ray being a very tall guy, leant back against the wall and nearly crushed him. Paul dived out of the way and that was the last communication I

The Jam

had with him'.

Bruce admits to being similarly upset over Paul's attitude: 'There's only so many birthday cards and Christmas cards you can send without getting an answer. I just don't understand that attitude'

So the prospect of a Jam reformation, though lucrative, remains highly improbable. The closest the band came was when the three musketeers played a gig on the same night. Unfortunately for Jam fans, it was three different gigs, with three different bands. So, at the moment, the nearest you might come is the American tribute band All Mod Cons.

What is important to Bruce and Rick, however, is to set the record straight on The Jam. Neither of them denies Paul Weller's status as one of the country's major songwriters.

'We all had just one thing we wanted to do. Any argument or disagreement we had, the importance of the group went over all of that. We managed to keep our motivation intact, right up until the split. And at the end the fans kept the motivation there, they didn't allow us to give up on them. It wasn't just Paul. We worked as a real unit, there was a genuine spirit to the band when it was going, and I think that depended on all three of us'.

'Yeh', adds Bruce, 'I think that's the most important thing. There were actually three people in The Jam. And two weren't Paul Weller'.

Acknowledgements

Alex Ogg would like to acknowledge the help given by the following people: Dawn and Doug for loan of archive material, Steve Smith, and David Lodge of 'Boys About Town'. BAT is an informative fanzine covering The Jam and Paul Weller. The magazine can be contacted via Dave at 5 Sherbrook Gardens, Dundee, Scotland, DD3 8LY. It is from this source that the material on Neil Harris and Steve Brookes was culled. Also thanks to Desktype of Cambridge and Bill and Marion.

Special thanks to Dawn Wrench for support and subsistence.

The Jam
UK Discography

SINGLES
In The City/Takin' My Love
Polydor2058 866   04/77

All Around The World/Carnaby Stree
Polydor2058 903   07/77

The Modern World/Sweet Soul Music/Back In My Arms
Again/Bricks And Mortar
Polydor2058 945   10/77

News Of The World/Aunties And Uncles/Innocent Man
Polydor2058 995   02/78

David Watts/'A' Bomb In Wardour Street
Polydor2059 054   08/78

Down In The Tube Station At Midnight/So Sad About
Us/The Night
PolydorPOSP 8   10/78

Strange Town/The Butterfly Collector
PolydorPOSP 34   03/79

When You're Young/Smithers-Jones
PolydorPOSP 69   08/79

Eton Rifles/See-Saw
PolydorPOSP 83   10/79

Going Underground/Dreams Of Children
PolydorPOSPJ 113   02/80
*(with free live EP featuring The Modern World/Away From The
Numbers/Down In The Tube Station At Midnight -
cat no 2816 024)*

Start/Liza Radley
Polydor2059 266   08/80

Funeral Pyre/Disguises
PolydorPOSP 257   05/81

Absolute Beginners/Tales From The Riverbank
PolydorPOSP 350   10/81

A Town Called Malice/Precious
PolydorPOSP 400   02/82

The Bitterest Pill/Pity Poor Alfie/Fever
PolydorPOSP 505   09/82

Beat Surrender/Shopping
PolydorPOSPJ 540   11/82
*(with free single featuring Move On Up/
Stoned Out Of My Mind)*

That's Entertainment/
Down In The Tube Station At Midnight
PolydorPOSP 482   01/83
(UK reissue of heavily imported European single)

Just Who Is The Five O'Clock Hero/The Great Depression
Polydor2059 504   01/83
(UK reissue of heavily imported European single)

NB: The entire roster of singles up to 'Going Underground' were reissued by Polydor in May 1980. The differences in design are slight, and can be established by comparing matrix numbers, label typography and wording, or the cut of the picture sleeve. Then in January 1983 all of The Jam's singles were reissued once more, this time with unlimited picture sleeves.

12" SINGLES
A Town Called Malice (live)/Precious (extended)
PolydorPOSPX 4000   02/82

Beat Surrender/Shopping/Move On Up/
Stoned Out Of My Mind
PolydorPOSPX 540   11/82

LPs
In The City
Polydor2383 447   05/77
Art School/I've Changed My Address/Slow Down/I Got By In Time/Away From The Numbers/Batman Theme/In The City/Sounds From The Street/Non-Stop Dancing/Time For Truth/Takin' My Love/Bricks And Mortar

This Is The Modern World
Polydor2383 475   11/77
The Modern World/London Traffic/Standards/Life From A Window/The Combine/Don't Tell Them You're Sane/In The Street Today/London Girl/I Need You (For Someone)/Here Comes The Weekend/Tonight At Noon/In The Midnight Hour

All Mod Cons
PolydorPOLD 5008   11/78
All Mod Cons/To Be Someone (Didn't We Have A Nice Time)/Mr Clean/David Watts/English Rose/In The Crowd/Billy Hunt/It's Too Bad/Fly/The Place I Love/'A' Bomb In Wardour Street/Down In The Tube Station At Midnight

Setting Sons
PolydorPOLD 5035   11/79

Girl On The Phone/Thick As Thieves/Private Hell/Little Boy Soldiers/Wasteland/Burning Sky/Smithers-Jones/Saturday's Kids/The Eton Rifles/Heat Wave

Sound Affects
PolydorPOLD 5035   11/80

Pretty Green/Monday/But I'm Different Now/Set The House Ablaze/Start/That's Entertainment/Dream Time/Man In The Corner Shop/Music For The Last Couple/Boy About Town/Scrape Away

The Gift
PolydorPOLD 055   02/82

Happy Together/Ghosts/Precious/Just Who Is The Five O'Clock Hero/Trans-Global Express/Running On The Spot/Circus/The Planner's Dream Gone Wrong/Carnation/Town Called Malice/The Gift

Dig The New Breed
PolydorPOLD 5075   12/82

In The City/All Mod Cons/To Be Somone/It's Too Bad/Start/Big Bird/Set The House Ablaze/Ghosts/Standards/In The Crowd/Going Underground/Dreams Of Children/That's Entertainment/Private Hell (all live)

Snap
PolydorSNAP 1   10/83

In The City/Away From The Numbers/All Around The World/The Modern World/News Of The World/Billy Hunt/English Rose/Mr Clean/David Watts/'A' Bomb In Waldour Street/Down In The Tube Station At Midnight/Strange Town/The Butterfly Collector/When You're Youung/Smithers-Jones/Thick As Thieves/Eton Rifles/Going Underground/Dreams Of Children/That's Entertainment/Start/Man In The Corner Shop/Funeral Pyre/Absolute Beginners/Tales From The

Riverbank/Town Called Malice/Precious/The Bitterest Pill (I Ever Had To Swallow)/Beat Surrender
Double album; Initial copies with free 'Live At Wembley' EP featuring The Great Depression/But I'm Different Now/Move On Up/Get Yourself Together
Polydor SNAP 45   *10/83*

Greatest Hits
Polydor849 554   06/91
In The City/All Around The World/The Modern World/News Of The World/David Watts/Down In The Tube Station At Midnight/Strange Town/When You're Young/The Eton Rifles/Going Underground/Start/That's Entertainment/Funeral Pyre/Absolute Beginners/A Town Called Malice/Precious/Just Who Is The Five O'Clock Hero/The Bitterest Pill (I Ever Had To Swallow)/Beat Surrender

Extras
Polydor513 772   05/92
The Dreams Of Children/Tales From The Riverbank/Liza Radley/Move On Up/Shopping/Smithers-Jones/Pop Art Poem/Boy About Town/A Solid Bond In Your Heart/No One In The World/And Your Bird Can Sing/Burning Sky/Thick As Thieves/Disguises/Get Yourself Together/The Butterfly Collector/Great Depression/Stoned Out Of My Mind/Pity Poor Alfie/Fever/But I'm Different Now/I Got You (I Feel Good)/Hey Mister/Saturday's Kids/We've Only Started/So Sad About Us/Eton Rifles/
(double album)

Wasteland
Pickwick 4129 P   10/92
News Of The World/Burning Sky/Saturday's Kids/Art School/In The Street Today/Non-Stop Dancing/Wasteland/In The City/Strange Town/Standards/'A' Bomb In Waldour Street/In The Crowd/London Girl/David Watts/I Got By In Time
Released on cassette and CD only

Dedications

From The Jam to all those who served...

Adoja, Chris	Security
Awome, Joe	Security
Bare, John	Rigger
Baron, Steve	Video Director
Bass, Peter	Lights Rigger
Batty, Bob	Lighting Rigger
Belcher, Alan	Original Roadie
Bell, Dickie	Tour Manager
Benson, Mike	Backline
Bucket, Mike	Coach Driver
Bush, Mel	Promoter
Chambers, George	Townhouse engineer
& Lonely	Townhouse dog
Coppersmith Heaven,	Producer
Vince Cox, Tim	Vapors Road Manager
Davidson, Walt	Photographer
De Boissiere, Phil	Lights
Elms, Paul	Truck Driver
Enfield Bance, Adrian	Driver
Fenton, Stuart	Lights
Fontaine, Claudie	Backing singer
Fuller, Colin	Lighting Designer and Operator
Gallagher, Maurice	A&R Polydor
Gibney, Tony	Security
Glanfield, Robby	Crew

The JAM

Harvie, Ian	Crew Boss
Hibbs, Trevor	Backline
Hill, Val	Catering
Hopewell, Martin	Agent
Jefferies, Bob	Monitors
Jones, Maurice	Promoter
Keedwell, Mike	Truck Driver
Liddle, Dave	Guitar roadie
Linch, Leonard	Coach Driver
Marnoch, Dougie	Lights
Miller, Wally	Drum Roadie
Morrison, Brian	Publisher
Munday, Dennis	A&R
Newman, Tony	Vapors Tour Manager
Nichol, Steve	Brass
Nicky	Original Roadie
Noble, Mike	Coach Driver (band)
Parry, Chris	A&R
Parsons, Tim	Promoter
Perry, Jeff	HEP Travel
Richards, Sue	Catering
Rickman, Simon	Lighting Rigger
Rounce, Tony	Crew
Ruffle, Pete	Truck Driver
Salter, Ray	Rigger
Sinden, John	Lighting Director
Telford, Jim	Keyboards
Thomas, Keith	Brass
Tinning, Neil	Photography
Tuck, Steve	Fly Man
Wheelen, John	Coach Driver (crew)
Wheeler, Caron	Backing singer
Wheeler, Kenny	Tour Manager/Security
Wick, Alan	Front Of House
Wilson, Pete	Engineer/Producer

Premiere	Drums
Vox	Amps
Marshall	Amps
Rickenbacker	Guitars

Pat and Lesley	For being there

Special thanks to Russell Emanuel & Dolphin Taylor

...and sorry to anyone we forgot!

Fan Club Details:
David Lodge
5 Sherbrook Gardens
Dundee
Scotland
DD3 8LY

Send SAE for details